CHOOSE
to
WORSHIP

A Journey of Intimacy with God

UZIEL G. GONCALVES

Edited by Beverly Hermans

DEDICATION

This book is dedicated to those who are seeking
every day for more and more of God, and to
those whose hearts are always burning
For His presence.

ACKNOWLEDGEMENTS

First of all, I thank God for choosing me for this project. He is the fount of all revelations inside this book. I couldn't do any of this without Him. I thank Him for continually touching my life with His love, and for guiding me in this journey of intimacy with Him through Worship.

To my wonderful wife Daniella, who never gave up on me and has been my support, my companion, my best friend, and my partner in this ministry of reconciling others with God through Worship. I love you, Dan, and always will. Our daughters, Rachel and Deborah, who are our portion from the Lord and always bring joy to our hearts, as they step in a lifestyle of worship.

To my parents, Joao and Estelita Goncalves, who raised me to be a servant of God. Their care, teaching and prayers made all diference in my life.

To my brother by choice Pastor Jailson Rocha and his wife Wanda Rocha from House of Healing Worship Center.

They've been my support in prayer. Their worship life has been an inspiration to me.

To Pastor Najem, who opened the doors of CCF Ministries for us, and the amazing CCF family, who welcomed us with open arms and love. From the moment we entered this family, a new season began in our lives, and this book is a proof of that.

To Beverly Hermans, who dedicated so many hours of her time editing this book, bringing my raw manuscript to life. I appreciate every comment you made in order to make it more refined. You and Stew have been a blessing in my life.

To my brother Saul Rodriguez, who designed the cover for this book. Thank you for blessing me with your talent.

ENDORSEMENTS

I so enjoyed reading *Choose to Worship*. The powerful testimonies and revelations the Lord has given Pastor Uziel in this book are so beautiful. As I read the book I could feel the Lord's heart for His people and His desire that we would experience the power of His love as we worship Him spirit and in truth. I so appreciate Pastor Uziel's honesty and humility. His willingness to write "real" is a powerful tool for the Lord to open hearts allowing the Holy Spirit opportunity to reveal the simple beautiful truths in this book. Every worship leader, every musician that ministers on a worship team and every Christian needs to read this book. Choose you this day whom you will serve, because He is God and worthy of it all!

Thank you Pastor Uziel for writing this book. God will use it to bring many back to the heart of worship!

Marlene J. Yeo
Director of Somebody Cares New
England and Lead Pastor of Community Christian
Fellowship of Haverhill

Thank you Uziel for your honesty and willingness to share your personal struggles and victories in the Lord, that plummeted you deep into the heart of God, where the Holy Spirit could bring forth worship from the very depth of your being, your heart.

Insightful teaching. Really reconfirming our focus. Worship is the Heart of the matter.

Rev. Elvira Whitcomb
Co-Founder and Co-Pastor of
CCF Ministries

What is worship? In his work *Choose to Worship*, Pastor Uziel G. Goncalves takes us through a journey of personal experiences and biblical insights of true worship. Goncalves dives into key aspects of the Christian life including spiritual warfare, personal holiness, and faith as components of biblical worship. Moreover, Goncalves concisely and meticulously deals with the biblical meaning of worshiping God in Spirit and Truth. A quick glance at the title of this book may lead many to believe that this work is only for worship leaders, however, this is a book that should be read by anyone interested in truly worshiping God.

Rev. Dr. Cecilio Hernández
Lead Pastor Iglesia
Cristiana Ebenezer Asambleas de Dios

I have read the book *Choose to Worship* by Pastor Uziel Goncalves who is a long time worshiper and a composer of music. The author's wife and their two beautiful daughters are all Church worshipers. The book is very helpful to the readers and especially those who are Church Worshipers. The book is rich in practical experiences from the life of the Anointed author. The book is relevance to our time, biblically and theologically sound. I recommend you to read this book and if you are a worshiper, this will enrich your skills and for others, the book will enlighten you more about the ministry of worship and probably it will give you a foundation and interest to explore your music and worship talent.

Bishop, David Karaya
BA, Mdiv. Edu CCF Ministries

CONTENTS

Foreword xv
Introduction xvii

The Concept of Worship 21
The Birth of Worship 24
Worship in Spiritual Warfare 34
Worship in Holiness 46
Worship in His Sovereignty 58
Worship in Faith 66
Worship His Way 74
The Power of Worship 85
Called to Worship 95

FOREWORD

F ew Christians really know true worship. Rev. Charles
Stanley once said that he believed "most Christians in
most churches have never worshiped God." We go to church,
but we don't worship. We sing songs, but we don't worship.
We listen to sermons, but we don't worship. All of these
things can be elements of the worship experience, but they
are not worship in and of themselves, which means that a
person can do all of them and yet fail to truly worship God.

We often mistake the means of worship for worship itself.
The Bible says "God is Spirit and those who worship Him
must worship Him in Spirit and in truth." Pastor Uziel is a
God chaser. He chases God through worship that rises from
his spirit by the Truth of the Word. Deep that calls to deep
is what true worship is. I have been blessed many times by
Pastor Uziel's worship; he burns a spiritual incense that
pleases the nostrils of Papa God. He has brought many com-
rades to prostrate themselves before God in worship. Pastor

Uziel, I am proud of you, a true man of God whose lifestyle
is the expression of worship. Great book.

Rev. Raffoul Najem
Founder and
Senior Pastor of CCF Ministries

INTRODUCTION

L ife is full of choices: good choices, bad choices, choices that we regret, choices that make us rejoice, choices that make us sad or mad, choices that we are persuaded to make, choices that we made on our own. We have choices to make with every step we take; every day we are pushed to make choices. All this brings us to one conclusion: we are the product of our choices. If we had made one different choice in the past, we would not be the same person we are today. Choices lead us to experiences we would never have had otherwise.

Another result of our choices is that they don't impact only our lives, but those of the people around us, and people who are led by God to meet us along the way.

When my wife, Daniella, and I decided to leave Brazil and come to the United States in the year of 2000, we knew our lives would never be the same. The experiences we went through, people we met from all over the world, friends we made, the two wonderful daughters God gave us here, the spiritual growth that occurred, the marriage troubles we faced here, and, by the grace of God, overcame, changed us forever. Today, we are who we are because of that one choice we made sixteen years ago, combined with all the choices we've been making every day in our lives since.

At the same time, we are assured that because of our decision to come to this country, we have had an impact on all the people we have met here.

I remember the day when I made the choice to not give up on my marriage. I thought that decision would affect just my wife and I, but time proved me wrong, and I will share one story in particular.

Daniella and I spent the whole year of 2001 struggling in our marriage, which almost ended up in a divorce, but in the beginning of 2002, right after we got back together and worked things out in our relationship, we decided to pursue God in a way we never had before. We realized that was the only way to restore our lives and our family. So we immersed ourselves deeply into the Holy Spirit. He was the missing link in our lives.

During this journey, we decided to open a Christian book store. After six months, we realized that financially the business was not a good investment, but we kept it going. In the next few months, one woman, who I'll call Deborah, began to frequent our store. As Daniella started to get to know Deborah better, we discovered she was a believer, but at that time was far from God. Daniella always talked to her about coming back to Jesus and prayed with her.

Time went by, we closed the store and lost contact with her, but five or six years later we spotted Deborah in one of the Brazilian churches in our city. After the service, Deborah told us how the time she spent in our store helped her to return to Christ. Immediately, God ministered to my spirit and said, "Your decision to continue to stay married to your wife made this. Your decisions affect other people's lives, not only yours." I realized that the only way to not mess things up for myself, the people around me, and people that I haven't even met yet, is to obey God. He knows our future, so He is the one who knows where our decisions will take us.

It may be difficult to understand how God knows everything: our past, present, and future; He knows our purpose of life. After all, He is the one who placed this purpose inside of us, and yet He gives us opportunities to fulfill it. He has never forced us and never will. One thing I now understand is that every time we make a decision without consulting God, we miss an opportunity to stay on His path to fulfill our purpose.

So, why *Choose to Worship*?

Worship is a journey of relationship, a journey of acknowledgement of God, a journey that can bring us back to Him, and to look like Him.

"Let us acknowledge the LORD; let us press
on to acknowledge him. As surely as the sun

*rises, he will appear; he will come to us like
the winter rains, like the spring rains that
water the earth." (Hosea 6:3)*

My invitation to you, through this book, is to come with
me on this twenty-four hours a day, seven days a week journey
of worship. Choose to Worship God, choose to be like Him.

Chapter 1

THE CONCEPT OF WORSHIP

*"Yet a time is coming and has now come when
the true worshipers will worship the Father in
spirit and truth, for they are the kind of worshipers the Father seeks."*   (John 4:23)

A s human beings, we have the tendency to conceptu-
alize everything around us. All we have experienced,
seen, eaten, and felt about these things are already formed
and stored in our brains.

Since I am a married man with two daughters, I have my
own views about marriage and fatherhood, because this is my
daily experience. When we talk about things we don't know,
we can only formulate ideas about them. People who have
never married, for example, have only a limited view about
marriage. People who don't know God have only a concept
of Him. Those who have never experienced the power of the

Holy Spirit have an opinion about Him based only on what they have heard, been taught or read about.

People who express their worship in an extravagant way can be open to criticism by those who believe we can't be respectful to God doing that. The problem is that when a person establishes a presupposition about how others worship God, that person can develop a judgment about those who worship God in a different way.

In 2011, my wife and I were organizing our church for a twenty-four-hour worship event with music, dance, prayers, etc. In our minds, we started to choose the people we believed were perfect to lead every two-hour shift. We looked for people who had the worship style we liked. A few weeks before the event, I had a dream, and in the dream Daniella and I were in Brazil (our home country). We were traveling to a church and arrived right when the worship team was about to start to play. As I entered the church, I realized that the song they were ministering was an old hymn book song.[1] As the group continued ministering, I thought in my heart, "How can this guy still sing this song? It's so old. I would never use this type of song to minister Worship." And right in that moment, the presence of Holy Spirit filled the place, and I saw everybody getting on their knees, crying in repentance. People were so overcome by the Holy Spirit. God's presence was so tangible that I couldn't help but fall on my knees, crying. Then I heard the Lord's voice whispering in my ear, **"True worship is not in your own conception, but in my**

Spirit." God used this dream to teach me what I needed to know but wasn't comprehending. I woke up and repented for every concept that I had formed about worship, and started to search and ask God to show me the meaning of being a True Worshiper.

Therefore, this book is not an attempt to define True Worship, but through the information presented, everyone may decide in their soul, to connect their spirit to God and, through His Truth become a True Worshiper. This is what God is seeking (John 4:23).

[1] I have nothing against these hymns I grew up singing. Now they have a much bigger impact in my life than it had 30, 35 years ago. I can express my love, my worship to God with them.

Chapter 2

THE BIRTH OF WORSHIP

"But you must not eat from the tree of knowledge of good and evil, for when you eat from it you will certainly die." (Gen. 2:17)

A dam was made as the crown of creation, who walked and talked with God every day, heard His voice clearly, and even though the Bible doesn't mention it, it suggests that Adam, before his sin, could actually see God. *"But your iniquities have separated you from your God; your sins have hidden His face from you."* (Isa. 59:2). How could Adam decide to rebel against God and His Word?

How could Lucifer, created to be the Model of Perfection, anointed as a guardian cherub, who lived on the mountain of God, decide to rebel against God?

This is a question I had since my teen years. I couldn't quite understand how these two would trade the splendor of

God's presence for a life with emptiness and darkness. Why is that?

The Bible indicates that, before the fall, Satan was an anointed cherub, named Lucifer, created to worship God with all his beauty, leading the angels under his command in the praises of the Lord. *"You were anointed as a guardian cherub, for so I ordained you. You were on the holy mount of God; you walked among the fiery stones. You were blameless in your ways from the day you were created till wickedness was found in you."* (Ezek. 28:14–15). Because of his pride Lucifer chose to rebel against God, thinking he could get all the glory and praises that are due only to God. Why is that?

God created mankind to fellowship with Him. Adam, having God's image and likeness, was created to worship God, knowing that He is the one who deserves all the glory and praises. Adam was responsible to lead all nature in praises to God. One day, Lucifer, the devil, placed in Adam's mind the desire to be like God by knowing good and evil. This consumed Adam's mind, and he chose to rebel against God, thinking he could do and receive everything that is due only to God. Why is that?

It is something that still can lead us to blessings or curses — it is our freewill. When man was formed, he received not only the image and likeness of the Godhead, but a vessel where He could dwell — the temple of our bodies. We received the functions that are executed in the spiritual realm of heaven. We understand that Michael, as the leader of God's army, without any thought, is always ready to execute God's commands. In the same manner, Gabriel delivers God's messages promptly, making a connection between humans and God. Unlike them, Lucifer was created to hold the glory and majesty of God, to lead his angels in worship. And this is not something that is executed right away without thinking.

God is love and, being love, He can't demand to be worshiped and loved by force. Being love, He can command that His word and His purposes be fulfilled. Like a CEO of a company, He can command his order to be executed, He can command his employees to work, but He can't command to be loved by his employees. The same way, our bodies are designed to operate in the physical world with all the functions working properly. Our nose can't hear anything, nor can our hands taste anything. Even if we would like it to be so, our bodies cannot do anything besides what they are designed to do, just like Michael the Archangel is ready to do what he is supposed to do. The same way, our spirits have no other function than making the connection between us and God, like Gabriel makes this connection through the messages he delivers. When we talk about our souls, we talk about our emotions, feelings, desires, love, hope, etc. We talk about freewill. So, loving God is something we choose to do. And because worship is an act of love, we will never worship Him if we don't choose to.

From the moment God told Adam not to eat from the tree of knowledge of good and evil or he would die, freewill was established not only in his life, but in ours too. We inherited the power of decision making to do things God's way or our way. This means, even though worship was created in God and by God, and it is He who places in our hearts the desire to worship Him, our worship is executed in our freewill. God seeks worshipers who worship Him in Spirit and Truth, and this journey starts in our decision to do so.

Making the decision to worship God is not enough to make us True Worshipers. The Bible doesn't say that a True Worshiper worships God in the soul, but in Spirit and Truth. It means that the soul is not capable to give God the real worship. We need something else to please God with our worship.

The story of Cain and Abel is a perfect example. *"Cain brought some of the fruits of the soil as an offering to the Lord. But Abel brought fat portions from some of the first-born of his flock. God looked with favor on Abel and his offering, but on Cain and his offering He didn't look with favor."* (Gen. 4:2–5).

They both had the desire to worship God, but if we take a closer look at the verses, we will see that God not only looked on the offerings, but on who brought the offerings. The desire to please God was born in the freewill of Cain and Abel, but only Abel was capable to achieve the task. Cain came only with his freewill. Abel came with something else. What was it? What did Abel's offering have that was so special?

When Jesus watched the crowd putting their money into the temple's treasury, He noticed that among all those people, a poor widow, who put in only a small offering of two copper coins, gave more than everyone. *"I tell you the truth, this poor widow has put more into the treasury than all the others."* (Mark 12:42).

Not only the widow, but everyone in that crowd had the desire to bring their offering to the temple's treasury. The difference between them is that they brought only their freewill characterized by their attitude about money, but the widow brought something else. What was it? What did her offering have that was so special?

True worship to God, who made everything that exists to be whole, can't be otherwise but whole. Jesus taught us that True Worship is the one that is in Spirit and Truth. There is no other way. We can try all different things; all different methods, all different words, actions, attitudes, but at the end, if it hasn't come through Spirit and Truth it will not please God. When God views our worship and doesn't see His Spirit, nor His Son in it, He doesn't see in us the wholeness of His own creation; therefore, this worship can't touch His heart. When He sees only the freewill, He sees the fall of the man, but how does God see Jesus and the Holy Spirit in true worship? What does it really mean to worship Him in Spirit and Truth? What is it to be a True Worshiper?

WORSHIP IN SPIRIT

In Genesis 5:3 we find that Adam, after 130 years, had a son in his own likeness, and his own image.

Adam, before he sinned, had the image and likeness of God the Father, the Son and the Holy Spirit. After his sin, the image and likeness that Adam transferred to his son wasn't the same one he received when he was created. His body, once imperishable, now will die and it will become dust. His spirit, once completely connected to God, is now totally separated from his creator. His soul, once full of love and all the attributes of God, is now full of sin: lies, envy, corruption, destruction. This is now the likeness and image Adam passed to his sons and daughters and to all generations, even to us.

Because we are born with the image and likeness of Adam, our spirits are separated from God. We are disconnected from Him—we cannot feel His presence. We cannot walk with Him in the garden and we cannot worship in spirit unless the connection between our spirit and His Spirit is reestablished. This happens when salvation takes place in our lives and we allow the Holy Spirit to dwell in us and work in our hearts, conforming us until the image and likeness of God, once again, is formed in us.

For a long time, I was intrigued by this verse: *"true worshipers will worship the Father in spirit and truth, for they are the kind of worshipers the Father seeks."* (John 4:23).

People generally connect worship to music because this is the way we have been taught and what we have experienced. Worship is so much more, as is stated so eloquently in the song *Heart of Worship*, God is searching for more than a song—He is looking deeper into our hearts. The Bible clearly shows this. *"For the eyes of the LORD range throughout the earth to strengthen those whose hearts are fully committed to him"* (2 Chron. 16:9).

"The LORD detests those whose hearts are perverse, but he delights in those whose ways are blameless." (Prov. 11:20).

"Above all else, guard your heart, for everything you do flows from it." (Prov. 4:23).

One of the characters in the Bible I really admire, and who is the perfect example of this, is Job. There is no Biblical record of Job using music, but God found him to be a true worshiper. God knew Job's heart and knew he would not fail, even in the midst of all the circumstances he went through. God testified about him. *"Have you considered my servant Job? There is no one on earth like him; he is blameless and upright, a man who fears God and shuns evil."* (Job 1:8).

It wasn't music that separated Job from God's other servants, but his *attitude*. I believe there were many in Job's time who sang songs and brought sacrifices to God, but no one else had Job's heart; no one else commanded God's attention in this way. Not many would be able to be like Job after what he suffered. *"Then he fell to the ground in worship and said: 'naked I came from my mother's womb, and naked I will depart. The Lord gave and the Lord has taken away; blessed be the name of the Lord."* (Job 1:20–21).

Music is just a tool that we can use to express our worship.

It is common in our churches to hear the expression "moment of worship," referring to the time when the worship team plays slow songs. That's when we see people closing their eyes, lifting their hands, feeling the song. This is a manifestation of the presence and the move of the Holy Spirit. Because He is God, He can pour down his gifts upon anyone, any time in any way He wants. I believe God directs us to express our worship with everything we have; voices, bodies, emotions, etc. This doesn't necessarily mean the people who receive and express the gifts are true worshipers. For God is not looking on the outside, to the emotion caused by the manifestation of the Holy Spirit, but He's looking into the heart. He's looking to the reaction in our lives caused by the *dwelling* of the Holy Spirit: the way we talk, walk, act and react in response to everything that happens to us.

Saul, when he was anointed King of Israel in Gibeah, *"A procession of prophets met him; the Spirit of God came upon him in power, and he joined in their prophesying."* (1 Sam. 10:10).

The Spirit of the Lord overtook Saul in such a way that everyone could see the manifestation of God's Spirit. He started to prophesy along with the prophets. Unfortunately, during his kingship, we see that the King's attitudes, his actions, his words and his thoughts didn't reflect someone who had his spirit connected to God, who had God's character forged in him; a spirit transformed by God's image and likeness.

Showing the manifestation of the Holy Spirit in your life, and living by the Holy Spirit, are two completely different things. It is wonderful to have the gifts of the Holy Spirit operating in our lives, but it is God's desire to have the Holy Spirit directing our lives in a way which can show His fruit in and through our lives.

WORSHIP IN TRUTH

No one except God and I know what is in my heart when I come before Him to worship, to pray, or just to stay in His presence. I can masquerade my intentions so others will think I'm coming in truth, but it is absolutely impossible to masquerade my feelings, desires, and thoughts to God. He knows my heart, like He knew Job's heart, Saul's heart, David's heart. I cannot hide anything from Him, especially whether the truth is in me or not.

What is the meaning of truth? In John 8:32 Jesus said, *"Then you will know the truth, and the truth will set you free."* Usually, people conveniently drop the first part of this verse and so misinterpret the second part, *the truth will set you free,* as if we tell the truth, it will set us free. If that were so, we could do anything wrong, tell the truth about what we did, and, bam! We would be free of all the consequences related to the wrong we did. Jesus didn't say, "then you will tell the truth," but "you will know the truth." Jesus also said, *"I am the way, and the truth, and the life. No one comes to the father except through me."* (John 14:6).

My whole Christian life, I heard a lot of messages about this verse, and in all of them the preachers talked only about salvation. Of course there is no other way to spend eternity with God, if it's not through Jesus. Also, there is no other way to come before God if it's not through Jesus, the Truth. It means, when we move towards God, it has to be through Jesus: our prayers through Jesus, our searching for His face through Jesus, our repentance through Jesus, our worship through Jesus. *"For there is one God and one mediator between God and men, the man Christ Jesus."* (1 Tim. 2:5). He is the truth, and without Him there is no way to worship in truth; without the blood of Jesus covering all discrepancies between our image and God's; Without living in truth—in Jesus—it is impossible to worship God in truth.

In our worship, God wants to see our free will always choosing Him, He wants to see our spirit connected to Him by his Holy Spirit, and He wants to see His son's blood covering our disobedience, our sin, our fall.

"A true worshiper worships God in Spirit and Truth."

Chapter 3

WORSHIP IN SPIRITUAL WARFARE

"As they began to sing and praise, the LORD set ambushes against the men of Ammon and Moab and Mount Seir who were invading Judah, and they were defeated." (2 Chron. 20:22)

W e are in the middle of a war whether we believe it or not—whether we want it or not. This war began before mankind was created. When Lucifer thought he could be worshiped like God, he declared war against God. The interesting thing is, because he knows his war is already lost, his main goal now isn't to destroy God's worshipers in the physical realm, but in the spiritual realm. More than trying to kill us, he is interested in deceiving us (tempting us to sin and disobey God.) The Devil is going to try everything in his arsenal of weapons to put us in a position where our actions in this physical realm will result in our spiritual death. It doesn't mean that he won the war against God, but it means that he won the war against us. He is transforming us into enemies of God, who, just like him, will have the same destiny: The Lake of Fire.

The story of King Jehoshaphat, described in 2 Chronicles 20, is one of the most amazing examples of how the power of worship can achieve victory over the enemy's attacks. Of course Jehosaphat's enemies were ready to battle a physical war against him and the kingdom of Judah, but God gives us spiritual applications for useful strategies, because, *"Our struggle is not against flesh and blood, but against the rulers . . . authorities . . . powers of this dark world . . . and spiritual forces of evil in the heavenly realms."* (Eph. 6:12).

> *"After this, the Moabites and Ammonites with some of the Meunites came to wage war against Jehoshaphat."* (2 Chron. 20:1).

Satan is always ready to come against us. He never gives up, and no matter the circumstances we are in, no matter the quality of relationship we have with God, Satan will come to attack us. Even though our battle is in the spiritual realm, he'll come against our physical world, believing that our physical suffering will weaken us spiritually: *"But stretch out your hand and strike everything he has, and he will surely curse* you *to your face"* (Job 1:11). Remember that his intention is to permanently destroy our spiritual relationship with God.

DON'T NEGLECT THE WARNINGS

"Some men came and told Jehoshaphat: A vast army is coming against you." (2 Chron. 20:2).

As much as Satan wants, he can't just come with his vast and powerful army of demons and destroy our spiritual relationship with God without warning us. You might be asking, "What do you mean, without warnings? Attacks happen unexpectedly—there is no warning." Remember that even though things happen in the physical realm, He is not after our bodies, but our souls. We receive warnings all the time, but in most cases, we don't see it, we don't feel it, we don't smell it, we don't hear it because we are not alert—we are only focused on the natural and physical realm. We don't live like we are in the middle of a war: a spiritual war. Sometimes we sense something—see it, feel it, smell it, hear it—but we don't know what to do. A man who cheated on his wife received a lot of warnings before the actual betrayal happened: a thought, a look, a flirting, a feeling, new emotions, and . . . too late! Ignoring these warnings can cause not only the destruction of a family, but God's purpose for them.

This is what always amazes me: God created us with a particular purpose in our lives, but He leaves it up to us to fulfill it. Every day we have a chance to do it or not; every choice we make defines our position and commitment to this purpose God placed in us.

BRING THE WARNINGS TO GOD

My wife and I came to this country in the year of 2000. We had been married for 6 years, and we were living the dream of living in the USA. About 10 months after we arrived, we started to have some troubles in our marriage. No one thought this could happen. The enemy came with his vast army and his vast arsenal of weapons against me. There were warnings. Thoughts about another woman started to grow in my mind; thoughts about how wonderful a marriage could be if I had married her and not Daniella. Instead of bringing these thoughts to God, I continued to ignore them, because they were exciting to me. The thought went to a conversation; from a conversation to a desire; from a desire to the decision to break up with my wife and go back to Brazil to marry that woman. Today I thank God I was in the United States at that time, otherwise the sin would have grown larger and it would have destroyed God's purpose in my life, my wife's life and that woman's life. It would have brought immense pain to me and my family.

In the middle of all this distress and discouragement, in the middle of this war that came as a bomb upon our lives, the decision that my wife made was what resulted in victory over the enemy and his army. She brought the warnings to God.

"God! Did you see this? The enemy is coming against my marriage and I can't do anything, but, if you talk like the people in the church say you talk, talk to me." The answer came right away when she opened the Bible. *"Perhaps the reason he was separated from you for a little while was that you might have him back forever."* (Philem. 1:15). This was the answer she needed. From that moment on she refused to give up on us, despite my contempt towards her.

The Bible says *"Cast all your anxiety on Him, because He cares for you."* (1 Pet. 5:7). This was exactly what Daniella did.

Every time we run to God showing Him the warnings of the attacks that are about to come, His answer comes. *" Then the Spirit of the Lord came upon Jahaziel . . . as he stood in the assembly. He said: Listen, King Jehoshaphat and all who live in Judah and Jerusalem! This is what the Lord says to you: Do not be afraid or discouraged because of this vast army. For the battle is not yours, but God's."* (2 Chron. 20: 14–15).

My wife knew the battle wasn't hers, but God's. Prayer and worship became her weapon. Even though she couldn't see the results immediately, in the physical realm, because of her prayers and worship, a spiritual war started not only against the demons that were trying to destroy our marriage, but also against me to convince me that I was wrong. She couldn't convince me, but the Holy Spirit could, for He is the one who has the power to convince us from our sins. *"When He comes, He will convict the world of guilt in regard to sin, and righteousness and judgment."* (John 16:8).

Our spiritual battle lasted one year. During that time many people spoke into my life trying to convince me that, as a Christian, I could not divorce my wife, but I didn't want to listen to anyone. I remember my pastor saying, "Uziel, I'm not going to show you through the Bible that you are wrong, because you know the Bible and you know you are wrong, but I can pray, and I can cry with you." And that was what he did.

So I decided to challenge God, and look for answers myself. I said. "God! If you want to talk to me, talk to me, but talk in a way that I can really hear. Don't send anybody to tell me I'm wrong. I know I'm wrong, but tell me why I cannot do what I'm doing. So many people get divorced, why can't I?"

God was waiting for that. He placed in me a desire for His word like I never had before. The first thing He did was to take me to *Ezekiel 3:10: "And He said to me, son of man, listen carefully and take to heart all the words I speak to you."* I started to spend hours reading my Bible. And every day I prayed this prayer that I learned from Benny Hinn in his book *Good Morning Holy Spirit:* "Good morning Holy Spirit! As I'm reading the book that you wrote, could you come and reveal to me what you mean through this Word?"

And He did! Every time I opened my Bible, something about divorce would come up, like:

> *"I hate divorce, says the Lord God of Israel."* (Mal. 2:16).

> *"The Lord is acting as the witness between you and the wife of your youth."* (Mal. 2:14).

> *"Moses permitted you to divorce your wives because your hearts were hard. But it was not this way from the beginning."* (Matt. 19:8).

Even though these were hard words for me at that time, the Holy Spirit always ministered to my heart, having me meditate on them and recognize the truth in each one of them.

Right after all these piercings of the sword of the Spirit about divorce hit my heart, God started to reveal His plans to my life. And one day when I was reading my Bible, I could understand His plans for me. It was there in Isaiah 61:1–3. It was like hearing the voice of God calling me to the pastoral ministry. With tears rolling down my face I started asking myself, "How can God call me for such a thing when I am doing things that He hates? I am not prepared for that. At that moment I felt so ashamed of the things I was doing, that I couldn't believe God wanted me as a minister. The answer came through verse six *"And you will be called priest of the Lord, you will be named minister of our God."* I had to decide to accept this call or continue doing what I was doing. I couldn't have both.

After a couple of days, I felt the strong voice of the Holy Spirit inside of me telling me, "Trust in me, I have a call for you."

The decision to trust in Him didn't come immediately; it came a few days before the date that I had planned to return to Brazil. I had asked God all morning for a reason why I couldn't just divorce my wife, marry again, and then follow his path. Maybe you are thinking, "What kind of question is that? How can you ask God to do your will first and then to do His?" It sounds weird, right? But it is the right thing to do when you are in the middle of confusion, indecision, and doubts. Go to God and talk to Him about all of these. After all, He made us, He knows us better then anyone else. The real problem is that many, many believers today don't want to hear God's opinion, nor do whatever He tells them to do.

The Holy Spirit took me to 2 Corinthians 6:3, and I could understand why I had to put all my will aside and do what God wanted me to do. *"We put no stumbling block in any-one's path, so that our ministry will not be discredited."*

How could I tell people to do God's will if I wasn't willing to do so? Who would give credit to my words? My words could say the truth, but my life would tell the opposite.

I decided to stay with my wife and follow God's plan for our lives. It wasn't easy. Feelings of regret came to my mind.

Battles between mind and faith, flesh and spirit caused a great struggle in my life. But in the midst of all that, I decided to trust God and what He had for me. So I started to do things that could help me stay firm in my decision. I joined the worship team, cultivated friends who had the same desire to do God's will, sought God more than ever, and brought all my thoughts captive to Jesus. After thirteen years, I can still say it was the best decision I ever made. Choosing God is always the best decision you can make. When you do that you are choosing to give Him worship.

The reason for this testimony is for you to understand that it doesn't matter in what area of your life the enemy comes to attack. When you hear, see, smell or sense the warnings about the attack, run to God and tell Him. After all, the attack comes against you, but the battle is not yours, it is His.

DO WHATEVER GOD SAYS

"Do not be afraid or discouraged because of this vast army. For the battle is not yours, but God's. Tomorrow march down against them . . . You will not have to fight this battle. Take your positions; stand firm and see the deliverance the Lord will give you." (2 Chron. 20:15b-17).

How come God told Israel not to fight? *"The LORD will be with you. Jehoshaphat bowed down with his face to the ground and ALL the people of Judah and Jerusalem fell down in worship before the LORD. Then some Levites . . . stood up and praised the LORD . . . with a very loud voice."* (2 Chron. 20:17b–19).

God told them not to fight, but He also told them to march down against the enemy, take their positions and stand firm. In reality, God is telling us to use the weapon of worship He equipped us with. In other words, trust Him. As mentioned at the beginning of this chapter, worship is the reason we are in the middle of this war, but it is also the weapon that we can use to allow God to destroy Satan's attacks in our lives. The verses above could be understood this way: Tomorrow, march down against them with *Worship.* "You will not have to fight this battle. Take your positions as *Worshipers;* stand firm in *Worship* and see the deliverance the Lord will give you." The deliverance comes in obedience, in submitting ourselves to the Lord. For me, this is worship.

Many misunderstand *James 4:7. "Submit yourselves to God. Resist the devil, and he will flee from you."* It is because they omit the first part of the verse, which is the most important part: Submit to God. It is impossible to resist the devil without complete submission to God. The devil will never flee from you if he doesn't see God in you. I understand this verse as *"Submit yourself to God* in Worship. *Resist the devil, and he will flee from you."*

Satan is after our worship, and every time we refuse to worship God, the devil steals it, and Satan's prize, not his victory, is our souls. A defeated soul.

Our worship makes us to be just like the person or thing we worship. The Bible confirms this. *"Those who make [idols] will be like them, and so will all who trust in them."* (Ps. 135:18). We become like what or who we worship. If our worship target is a famous singer, gradually we will emulate that personality; dress alike, talk alike, act alike. The more we worship that singer, adore him, the more we become like him or her.

I want to use this verse to explain how we can defeat the devil in our lives.

Satan is not focused on attacking God, for he knows it is impossible to overcome God's power. So, he focuses all his attacks against God's people. Even though our image is being transformed to be like Christ's, it is not yet fully formed; so it is not too difficult for the enemy to defeat us. *"For we have no power to face this vast army that is attacking us. We do not know what to do, but our eyes are upon you"* (2 Chron. 20:12).

But when we meditate on Psalms 135:18, we start to understand, like king Jehoshaphat, *"our eyes are upon [the LORD]."* By recognizing and declaring that He is the only one capable to defeat the army that comes against us, we can let God fight for us. The revelation I had from Psalms 135:18 taught me a different aspect of my worship—the power to restore the image and likeness of God in me. The only way we can defeat Satan's attacks in our lives is reconquering the image and likeness of God in us. And, the more we worship Him the more we become like Him. The more we worship Him the more of His image is reflected in and through us in such a way that when the devil comes after us, he sees God, who is undefeatable.

Worship is a powerful weapon, available for all of us, ready to be used. We just need to make a decision (choose) to use it.

"A true worshiper worships God in the midst of war."

Chapter 4

WORSHIP IN HOLINESS

*"Consecrate yourselves and be holy, because
I am holy."* (Lev. 11:44)

How can God urge us to be holy if He knows our sin nature, our brokenness, our messed up lives? This is an impossible task for us to do. How can He expect holiness from us?

For a long time, I thought it was impossible to be holy. After all we are human, we are sinners like Adam, inheriting his sin and, even after we receive Jesus, we still sin, still make mistakes.

My parents always taught me a Christian way to live my life, separating right from wrong in a biblical perspective, and because of the teachings I received from them I could say no to a lot of bad things in my life. When I was in middle and high school, I remember when some of my friends at school brought in adult magazines, and I I refused to look at them.

They picked on me in a sarcastic way, "Ah! you are the holy one." I used to be so embarrassed and tried to explain to them, "No! No! I'm not the holy one and I don't want to be, but my religion doesn't allow me to do that." I was taught to do the right thing because of religion, not because of the holiness required from God. The doctrines of my denomination kept me from doing things that I would regret today, and I praise God for what I was taught, but I don't remember any emphasis of the spiritual application of a change of heart. In this case, the *end* was right, but the *means* were totally wrong.

If God urges us, so imperatively, to be holy, why has the church avoided it for so long? We cannot say: *"That's for the Old Testament."* No! The New Testament tells us this also.

"Therefore, I urge you, brothers in view of God's mercy, to offer your bodies as living sacrifices, holy and pleasing to God—this is your spiritual act of worship" (Rom. 12:1).

"Who has saved us and called us to a holy lives..." (2 Tim. 1:9).

"Rather he must be hospitable, one who loves what is good, who is self-controlled, upright, holy and disciplined" (Titus 1:8).

*"For it is written: Be holy, because I am
holy."*   (1 Pet. 1:16).

*"But you are a chosen people, a royal priest-
hood, a holy nation."*   (1 Pet. 2:9)

"You ought to live holy and godly lives."
                                       (2 Pet. 3:11)

How did we miss it? I believe we've avoided the command to be holy because, in our minds, we thought it was
something we had to do on our own and we felt this was
an impossible task. To skip frustration, we simply stopped
teaching and preaching about it. We really missed the point
of this call.

"I am the Lord, who makes you holy." (Lev.20:8).

That's the point. When we discover that it isn't by our
efforts, but by the grace and the glory of our God upon us
that we become holy, we can teach, preach and say out loud,
"Let's be holy, for our God is holy!" We cannot be holy
because of religion, which is only an ideology and a set of
rules, but because God calls us and causes us to be. And if
He does so, it is because He knows we can be like Him again.
Despite our sin nature, our messed up lives, our brokenness,
we can be holy.

How can this be? God was, is and always will be holy. Nothing can change that. It is His nature to be holy; our nature is unholy. The only way for us to become holy is to enter into the atmosphere of holiness, which means to enter into the atmosphere of God. Even though it is God who makes us holy, it's our decision, our choice to be holy. Once again, it is our freewill. Once we are in God's holy atmosphere, His glory will turn everything that is in Him to be just like He is—holy. The same way, if we leave this atmosphere of God, He will continue to be holy, but we, far from Him, will return to our unholy nature. *"And there I will meet with the children of Israel, and the tabernacle shall be sanctified by my glory."* (Ex. 29:43 KJV). The more we get involved in the atmosphere of God's glory, the more He makes us holy. There's no way to find holiness in any place other than God. We can try everything. Nothing will make us holy but God.

THE MEASUREMENT OF HOLINESS

Is there a measurement of holiness that determines how holy we have to be? Is there such thing?

God commands us to be holy, but He doesn't say how holy we have to be. Honestly, I don't think there is a way to scale our holiness, but of one thing we can be sure. There is a way to know if we are or are not in the path of holiness. It is not for us to look at others to judge their ways and their attitudes, but to look at ourselves and see if there is something dragging us away from the the atmosphere of holiness. This has to do with being aware of the warnings detailed in the previous chapter.

I am totally fascinated by God's efforts to restore the relationship between Him and humankind, and once again give us the ability to walk with Him the same way Adam walked with Him in the Garden. From the beginning He designed us to be in a relationship with Him and it started with the promise He made right after Adam's fall. He promised Jesus Christ, who, unlike Adam, would defeat the devil, preparing for us a way to be in God's presence again, forever. Between God's promise and the actual birth of Jesus, and His victory over sin and death, a lot of things happened, but God never gave up on us. He always looked for a way to commune with us.

When God ordered Moses to build the Tabernacle, He was in effect saying: I want to live among my people, I want to fellowship with them again. The Tabernacle will provide a way for my people to return to relationship with me.

The word Tabernacle comes from the Hebrew verbal root *Sakhan*, which means "temporary dwelling," a shadow of the one that is in heaven.

> *"The Most High does not live in houses made*
> *by men."*   (Acts 7:48)

> *"Heaven is my throne and the earth is my foot-*
> *stool. Where is the house you will build for me?*
> *Where will my resting place be?"* (Isa. 66:1)

> *"They served at a sanctuary that is a copy and*
> *shadow of what is in heaven."* (Heb. 8:5)

It is also a model, set by God, for His permanent resi-
dence—us. *"Do you not know that your body is a temple of*
the Holy Spirit, who is in you, whom have received from God?
(1 Cor. 6:19–20). We, as temples of the Holy Spirit, need
to live our lives according to the model given to Moses by
God Himself. *"Make this Tabernacle and all its furnishings*
exactly like the pattern I will show you." (Ex. 25:9).

Before it had been filled by God's glory, the Tabernacle
was anointed with oil and consecrated to God. Everything in
it was made holy, purified to be of service in God's house.
Nothing unclean could enter.

That is how we need to present ourselves before God as
a holy instrument, a holy utensil, purified and consecrated to
God, to be used for His glory. At the same time, in order to
be filled by His glory, our bodies (His Temple), need to be
washed by the blood of Jesus Christ, anointed with the oil
of the Holy Spirit, and consecrated to Him through our own
choice. A dirty temple cannot be filled with His holy presence.
In the same way, in a temple filled with His holy presence,
there is no place for filth.

The Bible shows us this in two different situations. When Nadab and Abihu (sons of Aaron), serving as priests in the Tabernacle brought unauthorized, unholy fire before God, they were consumed by fire that came from God's presence (see Leviticus 10:10). The Tabernacle had already been filled by the Glory of God— *"Then the cloud covered the Tent* of Mee*ting, and the glory of the Lord filled the Tabernacle."* (Ex. 40:34). Moses had anointed every utensil, every piece of furniture as well as Aaron and all his sons, consecrating them to ministry before God. Nothing unclean was to enter the Tabernacle. God was very straight with His orders, and He doesn't negotiate His principles. As soon as Nadab and Abihu entered the place filled with God's presence with impure hearts, trying to do God's work in a manner that didn't glorify Him, they were consumed by the fire of God who said, *"Among those who approach me I will show myself holy; in the sight of all the people I will be honored." (Lev. 10:3).*

Leviticus 10:10 says, *"You must distinguish between the holy and the common, between the unclean and the clean."* Every time the people offered a holy sacrifice, as God instructed them in Leviticus, chapter 1, fire <u>from the Lord</u> would come and consume the burnt offering (see *Leviticus 9:24*). But Aaron's sons took censers, <u>put fire in them</u> (works) <u>and added incense </u>(unauthorized). Disobedience and pride of their own work (like Cain) caused impure hearts.

If our actions, as ministers of God, don't honor Him, He still will be honored by His actions among us.

The book of Samuel, chapter two, tells us about Hophni and Phinehas, sons of Eli, the High Priest. Like Nadab and Abihu, they didn't honor God nor the offerings in their duties as priests. They were corrupt, using their positions as priests for their own benefit. Though they ministered to God with impure hearts, they were not consumed by God's fire like Nadab and Abihu. Why? Because even though the Ark of the covenant was there, the fire of God's presence wasn't, because of the impurity inside the Tabernacle. How could they be consumed by something that wasn't there? The more we are filled with impure things, the less His presence will be with us.

We need to live our lives in such intimacy with God that any unclean word, any unclean feeling, any unclean attitude, any unclean thought that comes to our minds will be consumed by the fire of God's presence in our lives. Yes, anything.

If we don't have this kind of life, it's not too late to get on track. Do you remember the story of king Hezekiah (see *2 Chronicles* 29) and how he promoted the purification of the Temple? It shows that the most important thing we need to have to walk toward God is the desire to do so. Again, our freewill. As the birth of our worship is in our freewill, freewill also is the place where a walk with God starts. The Temple had been closed up by Hezekiah's father, Ahaz. *"They also shut the door of the portico and put out the lamps. They didn't burn incense or present any burnt offerings at the sanctuary to the God of Israel."* (2 Chron. 29:7).

King Hezekiah's plan was to reverse every one of the things that were caused by his father and previous king, Ahaz. Hezekiah's intention was to bring back the presence of God to His Temple. If we have experienced the lack of His presence, that's where we need to concentrate our efforts—to restore His presence in us.

"In the first month of the first year of his reign, [Hezekiah] <u>opened the doors of the temple</u> of the Lord and repaired them." (2 Chron. 29:3).

We can definitely see the decision of king Hezekiah to open the doors of the temple. Despite the influence of his father, who did everything wrong in God's eyes, Hezekiah decided to reestablish the covenant with God. It was one of the first things he did after he began to reign. Hezekiah was raised in a wicked place, full of idolatry, but that wasn't an excuse to keep him from seeking God. It took his courage, decision, and determination to finally turn himself and his people to God.

With the doors opened, king Hezekiah assembled the priests and the Levites and told them to enter the temple and purify it. Everything that didn't belong to the temple nor hadn't been consecrated to be used in the temple needed to be thrown out. The temple could not be used as a place of sacrifices and offerings to the LORD if it still was an unholy place, full of unclean utensils, full of idols.

Hezekiah appointed the Priests and the Levites to do the task of purifying the Temple, but not before they themselves had been purified and sanctified before the Lord. The task of purifying the Temple could not be performed by anyone other than them. They were set apart by God as the only ones who could minister and do the work inside the temple. Nothing inside the temple could be touched or handled by others. If that happened, that utensil was considered unholy, and needed to be purified to be used in the temple again.

We are the temple of the Holy Spirit, the place where True Worship should be continuous. This will happen only if we worship God's way—the way He showed us in the Tabernacle of Moses, the Temple of David and the Temple of Solomon. To fulfill the task for worship that God created us for, we need to walk in this atmosphere of holiness. The thing is, if we start to allow unauthorized and unclean thoughts and desires, our own will, and all kind of sins to be placed and stored inside our temples, we are closing the doors of intimacy with God.

King Hezekiah didn't let the circumstances he grew up with conform him to the evil around him. He decided to change things, to have the temple cleansed so he and his people could once again worship God. *"When the offerings were finished, the king and everyone present with him knelt down and worshiped."* (2 Chron. 29:29). Then he experienced the will of God for himself, his people and his kingdom.

Like king Hezekiah, first we need to decide to be cleansed. We have to decide to allow God's Word to get inside our spirits to purify our minds and bodies. We need to decide to put an end to every unclean thing that is inside of us, restoring our temple to purity and holiness to be used again in true spiritual worship of God to bring glory and honor to Him.

> *"Therefore, I urge you, brothers, in view of God's mercy, to offer your bodies as living sacrifices, holy and pleasing to God—This is your spiritual act of worship. Do not conform any longer to the pattern of this world, but be transformed by the renewing of your mind. Then you will be able to test and approve what God's will is—His good, pleasing and perfect will."* (Rom. 12:1–2).

I don't know your past, the circumstances of what you had to go through during your childhood. I don't know the battles that you still have to fight. I don't know your hidden, unholy secrets that create a barrier that doesn't allow your worship to flow. But one thing I can tell you. It is not easy, but . . . Take your position, don't let yourself be defined by all the bad and negative things that happened to you. Decide to change your circumstances. Let the Word of God cleanse you and wash away all the unholy utensils inside of you. Fill your body, your mind, your spirit with worship to God and you will taste and prove how good, pleasing and perfect is the will of God, not only for you, but for those around you, too.

"A True Worshiper worships God in Holiness."

Chapter 5

WORSHIP IN HIS SOVEREIGNTY

"The Lord has established his throne in heaven,
and his kingdom rules over all" (Ps. 103:19)

HE RULES OVER EVERYTHING

I n this chapter, I won't cover God's sovereignty, because there is no question about that. As Psalms 103:19 says, "His kingdom (in which He is king) rules over all": everything, everyone, every spiritual being, every living creature on the face of the earth in the ocean or in the air, every star, every galaxy. The whole universe operates under His commands, nothing is out of His control. Instead, I will focus on our attitudes toward Him and His sovereignty; our acceptance or not of His lordship over us. This will define who we really worship.

Since the beginning, Satan—the devil—has been trying to convince us through his lies that since we were created in

God's image and likeness, that we have the same ability and power to be sovereign over our destiny. Many people, even Christians, believe this lie.

Satan might whisper, "You don't need God. He wants to hold you back from your full potential. You know what is best for yourself." But the reality is, the more we distance ourselves from God's will, the more we lose His image and likeness, and the less we become like Him. Our likeness to God is conditional to our obedience to Him. If we live a life of disobedience, it means His attributes are not in us, and if we don't have His attributes we'll never look or be like Him.

In our sin, we want His power—power to control, power to decide, power to be great in our own, power to be recognized as big achievers.

Imagine Eve, hearing all the words Satan told her, *"For God knows that when you eat (of the fruit) your eyes will be opened, and you will be like God . . ."* (Gen. 3:5). Imagine all the doubt that came through her mind about God's word; imagine all the excitement in her heart about knowing everything just like God does; all the things she could do; how great she could be. These are the same doubts and excitement that come through our minds and hearts still. But don't be deceived like Eve, for the only achievement we can get with disobedience is death.

"But you must not eat from the tree of the knowledge of good and evil, for when you eat from it you will certainly die." (Gen. 2:17).

As we read through the Bible, we see that whenever anyone tried to get the glory for themselves, God struck him down. Is it because He is a cruel God? A tyrannous God? No. Not at all, but because He is a loving God he doesn't want us to remain in a lost condition, for He knows what pride can do. *"And this is the will of Him who sent me, that I shall lose none of those he has given me, but raise them up at the last day"*. (John 6:39).

Lucifer once was great in God's kingdom, carrying the glory of the Lord wherever he was; in his body all the sounds of instruments were made. It was like they were built inside of him. All the rhythms, melodies, everything concerning music was in him to glorify God's name. Because of everything he was, everything he had, in his heart he decided he was like God. A creation will never be like its creator. All creation has limitations that will never be overcome. Pride makes us think we are on a higher plane than everyone else, causing us to feel that we have the right to be worshiped. That was what happened to Lucifer, and for that he received his fate. *"And for this he was driven in disgrace from the mount of God."* (Ezek. 28:16).

That is why the devil is always after us, wanting to bring us down to the same destiny he has. The proud man or woman never accepts the lordship of the LORD. That's why *"God opposes the proud, but shows favor to the humble."* (James 4:6). Worship is an act of humbleness, placing the object or person of our worship on a higher plane than ourselves.

God doesn't share His glory with anyone. *"I am the Lord; that is my name. I will not give my glory to another or my praise to idols."* (Isa. 42:8). This is not because He is afraid of competition, but because He is LORD. He is the only one who deserves the glory, and He will get what is due to Him and to His name.

> *"For thine is the kingdom, the power, and the glory, forever and ever, amen."*
>
> (Matt. 6:13 KJV)

When we accept God's sovereignty, we are recognizing that we are His creations, made to carry His glory. Nothing we do can change that fact. But our attitudes toward God will define if we are fulfilling His purpose in our lives. Every time we decide to accept His way, His will, His sovereignty over our desires, our thoughts, our plans, our ways, His name is glorified. For He said, *"For I know the plans I have for you,"* declares the Lord, *"Plans to prosper you and not to harm you, plans to give you hope and a future."* (Jer. 29:11).

HE OWNS EVERYTHING

Another aspect of God's sovereignty is in the fact that as a king, He not only rules everything, but He owns everything—for this is the right of kingship according to *I Samuel 8:10–17*. *"Samuel told all the words of the Lord to the people who were asking him for a king. He said: This is what the king who will reign over you will do: He will take your sons and make them serve with his chariots. Some he will assign to be commanders of thousands and commanders of fifties, and others to plow his ground and reap his harvest, and still others to make weapons of war and equipment for his chariots. He will take your daughters to be perfumers and cooks and bakers. He will take the best of your fields and vineyards and olive groves and give them to his attendants. Your menservants and maidservants and the best of your cattle and donkeys he will take for his own use. He will take a tenth of your flocks, and you yourselves will become his slaves."*

"The earth is the Lord's, and everything in it,
the world, and all who live in it." (Ps. 24:1).

No matter what we do or how hard we try to own and get control of our lives, we belong to Him. The fact that everyone belongs to Him doesn't mean He will keep us all. Think about the things you possess. You will not keep everything. Some things you destroy, some things you give away, some things you trade; but you keep some things that you have a real connection with. Why we always think that when it comes to God it has to be different? Mark 8:34 says *"If anyone would come after me, he must deny himself and take up his cross and follow me."* This is the key. We all want to be with Him, so we need to submit ourselves to Him.

"For from Him and through Him and to Him are all things. To Him be the glory forever! Amen." (Rom. 11:36). It is just a matter of accepting or not accepting the fact that we, and all the things we have, belong to Him for His glory.

The Bible also says Jesus is King of kings and LORD of lords (see Rev. 19:16). This means not only everything that exists in every kingdom belongs to Him, but He gives us the option to surrender everything he put in our hands for us to use. Surrender our lives to in order to receive the citizenship of His kingdom, or, we could deny his kingship, refuse to surrender, and be treated as citizens of the defeated kingdom— the kingdom of darkness.

As believers, we were rescued from the dominion of darkness and brought into the kingdom of the Son He loves, according to Colossians 1:13. From the moment we receive Christ, we have to live according to the rules of God's kingdom. Once we are brought to God's kingdom, we can't live our lives with the same rules and principles of the dominion of darkness. Those who insist on living by those rules and principles will be destroyed, just like their ruler, the devil. *"And the devil, who deceived them, was thrown into the lake of burning sulfur, where the beast and the false prophet had been thrown. They will be tormented day and night forever and ever."* (Rev. 20:10).

> *"If anyone's name was not found written in the book of life, he was thrown into the lake of fire."* (Rev. 20:15).

HE IS NOT ONLY OUR SAVIOR, HE IS OUR LORD

When an angel of the Lord appeared to the shepherds to announce the birth of Jesus, he said to them, *"Today in the town of David a savior has been born to you; he is Christ the Lord."* (Luke 2:11).

It is impossible to say that Jesus is our savior if we don't receive Him as our Lord, because the Lord became savior, and not the other way around. We like to think of Him just as our savior, who is compared to a lamb who was slain and didn't open his mouth. He didn't ask anything from us to become our savior, He just gave himself up. He chose to become like me and you, He chose to become sin and a curse, to suffer and to die. Jesus said this about Himself in John 10:17–18, *"The reason my Father loves me is that I lay down my life, only to take it up again. No one takes it from me, but I lay it down of my own accord. I have authority to lay it down and authority to take it up again. This command I received from my Father."*

The door of salvation was opened with His death and resurrection. It is easy to accept Him as our savior. We only need to believe in Him. *"They replied, believe in the Lord Jesus, and you will be saved . . ."* (Acts 16:31). To receive Him as Lord is not so easy, because it requires unconditional submission from us, and more than that, submission by love.

Those who receive Him as Lord are compared to the slave who was set free but decided to continue serving His Lord. *"But if the servant declares, I love my master and my wife and children and do not want to go free, then his master must take him before the judges. He shall take him to the door or the doorpost and pierce his ear with an awl. Then he will be his servant for life."* (Ex. 21:5–6). Because of our love for Him, we are His servants for life. This love for Him is based on the fact that He loved us first. *"We love because He first loved us."* (1 John 4:19).

The beauty in all of this is that we were slaves of sin, but he redeemed us. Now, instead of forcing us to do whatever He says, He set us free to choose to stay or go. Even knowing all the suffering He would endure, He chose to die to give us our freedom back. He doesn't impose His will on us, but He expects from us the same word that came out of apostle Peter's mouth, *"Lord, to whom shall we go? You have the words of eternal life."* (John 6:68).

"A true worshiper worships God in His sovereignty."

Chapter 6

WORSHIP IN FAITH

*"And without faith it is impossible to please
God, because anyone who comes to him must
believe that he exists and that he rewards
those who earnestly seek him."* (Heb. 11:6)

I believe God placed this chapter in my heart because, as a
musician for 37 years and "worship leader" for 13 years,
I've seen so many people who are part of a "worship team"
and yet haven't learned how to live a life of worship. It is
simply because they didn't learn how to live by faith.

What does faith have to do with worship?

Everything! If our prayers, if our worship, if our work
in the ministries, if our gathering on Sundays; in fact, if our
whole Christian lives are not driven by faith, we are fooling
ourselves and living a false Christianity. *"For we live by faith,
not by sight."* (2 Cor. 5:7). Since the Bible tells us that it is
impossible to please God without faith (see Hebrews 11:6),

this means that we won't be able to please God with our talents, our fasting and sacrifices if they are not driven by faith.

After the fall, we lost our ability to interact with the spiritual realm; our lives were reduced to live in this physical realm where everything is driven by sight. Anything that is not in the range of our five senses became unreal and unbelievable for us.

It is so easy to live by sight. We don't need to believe in anything except our senses. We can see, hear, touch, smell, and taste. These things are real and powerful enough for us to make decisions for every aspect of our lives. However, even though we can't use our physical senses in the spiritual realm doesn't mean they're not real. Faith is the key to enter into this realm where none of our physical senses work, because the only way for us to see, feel, hear, smell, and taste is by faith. *"Taste and see that the Lord is good . . ."* (Ps. 34:8) *"Now* faith *is being sure of what we hope for and* certain of what we do not see."* (Heb. 11:1).

I remember one day in our former church when Daniella and I were in a mid-week service and a pastor from Brazil was leading in worship through songs. In the middle of worship, a woman who we knew, entered the church and stood one row behind us. As soon as she settled, we began to smell this fragrance of oil; strong, but at the same time so good. We thought it was the woman's perfume. But not everyone in the church could smell this. We learned this woman could not use any perfume at all because of a skin allergy. Later on she said, "When I started to worship, I lifted my eyes and saw an angel with a vessel full of oil. The angel started to pour down the oil on me, which had a very strong and beautiful scent." Everything was real, but not caught by physical senses; otherwise, everyone in the service could have seen and smelled this. We couldn't see the angel, but we could smell the oil, and it was very real.

According to Hebrews 10:38, we need to live by unending faith. *"But my righteous one will live by faith. And I take no pleasure on the one who shrinks back."* God is not suggesting it; He is commanding it. To better understand this verse, we could explain it this way: Those who are justified by the faith in Jesus must live by this same faith; God takes no pleasure in those who go back to the life lived by sight. The same faith by the Holy Spirit that opened up our eyes and heart to receive Jesus must be the generator and operator that moves our lives. *"For in Him we live and move and have our being . . ."* (Acts 17:28)

It is by faith that we can look at ourselves and see righteousness. *"Therefore, there is now no condemnation for those who are in Christ Jesus, because through Christ Jesus the law of the Spirit who gives life has set you free from the law of sin and death."* (Rom. 8:1). God sees righteousness in us when we obey His word. *"Don't you know that when you offer yourselves to someone to obey him as slaves, you are slaves to the one whom you obey—whether you are slaves to sin, which leads to death, or* to obedience, which leads to righteousness?" (Rom. 6:16).

Why is living by faith so imperative in our lives? Why does God insist on it?

Genesis 3:6 explains it. The moment that changed human life forever happened because of one thing: physical sight. *"When the woman saw that the fruit of the tree was good for food and pleasing to the eye, and also desirable for gaining wisdom, she took some and ate it . . ."*

When we are driven by sight, we sin.

The moment we gave our lives to Jesus, we started a new life. One not guided by our brain, but by our faith. This means that we make no decision based on our human senses, but on our spiritual senses, which are guided by the Holy Spirit. Every person listed in the Hall of Faith of Hebrews Chapter 11 lived like this. Of course they made mistakes, of course they weren't perfect, but they learned how to walk and live by faith. Their prayers, their worship, their talk, their actions, their lives surely pleased God, because they became driven by faith.

How can we achieve this kind of faith?

We all agree that faith is a gift from God, according to I Corinthians 12:9, and something we receive from the moment we open our hearts to Jesus. Faith is not stagnant, but something that is growing, something that needs to be fed every day. This only can happen through a relationship with Jesus, the *"author and finisher of our faith."* (Heb. 12:2). Like any kind of relationship, it needs desire from both parties. Since God is so willing to have a relationship with us, then it is up to us to start and keep the relationship going and growing. *"Therefore tell the people: This is what the LORD Almighty says: 'Return to me,' declares the LORD Almighty, 'and I will return to you,' says the Lord Almighty."* (Zech. 1:3).

> *"Come near to God and He will come near to you."*　　　　　(James 4:8)

There is our freewill–again. There will be no growing faith if we don't decide to have it and nurture it.

There is something I call "The Cycle of Faith" to help us to increase our faith. It starts with our decision to hear, read, seek, and meditate in the Word of God.

> *"Consequently, faith comes from hearing the message, and the message is heard through the word about Christ."*　　(Rom. 10:17).

If we ask anybody if they have faith, the answer will probably be yes. It doesn't matter in who or what they have faith, but the fact is that there is only one true faith. *"There is one body and one Spirit . . . one Lord, one* faith, *one baptism."* (Eph. 4:4–5). And this only true faith comes by hearing the Word of God. The Word produces faith and faith leads us back to the Word. If this is not true in our lives, something is wrong. If your faith doesn't lead you to the Bible, it is not a true faith. The same way, if the source of your faith is not the Bible, it is not a true faith. This is how this Cycle of Faith works: the more we hear the Word, the more our faith grows and the more our faith grows, the more we seek to hear and obey the Word.

Another aspect of faith that is necessary to understand is that without deeds our faith is dead. *"As the body without the spirit is dead, so faith without deeds is dead."* (James 2:26).

For a very long time I thought that this verse was related to the good deeds we do to others. Christians do need to help others in need, but a true faith cannot be related, nor only defined by, an act of kindness. It has to be more than that.

> *"You foolish person, do you want evidence that faith without deeds is useless? Was not our father Abraham considered righteous for what he did when he offered his son Isaac on the altar? You see that his faith and his actions were working together, and his faith was made complete by what he did."*
> (James 2:20–22).

There was no act of kindness by Abraham in that moment. There is only an act of obedience, which is nothing more than faith in action. This is what caused the big difference in Abraham's life. His faith was complete, not because of what he said or believed, but because of what he did, which always has been proof and confirmation of belief. It doesn't matter if I say I believe Jesus can save and transform any situation in my life, if my actions in the midst of troubles say a different thing. When Abraham was asked by God to sacrifice Isaac, he knew that, even if Isaac had to die, God would be able to resurrect him. Abraham's action was based on the promise God had made to him years ago, that through Isaac, he would be a father of nations. Therefore, Isaac would never die without having a son.

Our beliefs can only be sustained by our actions.

Why do we see so many Christians today, acting so differently than what the Bible teaches? Why don't so many Christians stand up for what the Bible says? The culture of America is becoming so politically correct that, in order to not offend anyone, nothing can be called sin. Our nation's opinions and points of view are no longer based on God's Word, but on worldly belief system.

The truth of Romans 12:2 is no longer tolerated. *"Do not conform any longer to the pattern of this world, but be transformed by the renewing of your mind . . .."*

Some believers have believed this lie so much so that the difference between believers and nonbelievers is no longer seen. Both think the same, act the same, profess the same ideologies.

How can we, as believers, sustain our faith with our actions, if our actions are not supported by our faith?

Everything we think, everything we say, everything we do collectively determines what kind of faith we have. *"And without faith it is impossible to please God, because anyone who comes to Him must believe that He exists and that He rewards those who earnestly seek Him."* (Heb. 11:6).

Usually the Church only associates faith with prayers, miracles, promises, and prophecies. She also surmises that our faith only needs to be exercised when we are in the midst of troubles and difficulties. Most forget that everything done without faith won't please God: prayer, dance, song, lifting up hands and voices to God, church attendance every Sunday, serving in the church, even living a Christian life, which involves all these things—without faith—won't please God. Worship without faith definitely won't please God.

Worship is not merely singing or lifting hands, it is not a dancing act, or playing instruments. You can do all these things, and more, and still won't get it right if not driven by faith—a life driven and guided by the Word of God. Obedience will lead you to righteousness before God (obedience is the manifestation of faith), which pleases God. Coming before God and trying to worship Him without a life of obedience is foolishness, and it will never please Him.

"A True Worshiper worships God in Faith."

Chapter 7

WORSHIP HIS WAY

*"Then have them make a sanctuary for me, and
I will dwell among them. Make this tabernacle
and all its furnishing exactly like the pattern I
will show you."*   (Ex. 25:8–9)

When I meditate on this verse, I recognize that it is
our bodies that are sanctuaries of the Holy Spirit
which should be exact copies of the pattern of the heavenly
sanctuary. They need to be filled according to God's instruc-
tions; in fact, when God created us to be His sanctuary on
Earth, He replicated in us His spiritual DNA. Everything in
us, everything on us, and everything through us must reveal
the glory of the dwelling place of our God. The worship that
flows from our lives must be connected and must be a con-
tinuation of the worship that occurs before the throne of God
in heaven, led by the Holy Spirit. What is the connection
of being led by the Holy Spirit and about our freewill of

choosing to worship? Because once we make the decision and set in our heart to worship God in everything, the Holy Spirit takes the lead in guiding us into the ways of worship. When our freewill makes room for the Spirit, wherever the Spirit goes we go; whatever the Spirit says we say; whatever the Spirit does we do. It is impossible for us to truly worship God on our own. Worshiping God is something that happens in the spiritual realm, so it is necessary the work of the Holy Spirit reconnecting us in this realm and guiding us into this path of worship.

Worship brings God's presence. Even though He is omnipresent, His manifested presence dwells in the midst of praises and worship. *"But you are holy, O you that inhabits in the praises of Israel."* (Ps. 22:3). Ushering in His presence is something that cannot be done according to our under-standing. It needs to be done His way. Without a doubt, we are responsible to prepare the place of His dwelling—just like the people of Israel prepared the Tabernacle in the middle of the desert or like Solomon who built the Temple according to the plans God had given to David (see 1 Chronicles 28:19). God is the one who determines how places must be prepared. It's His way, not ours. These places of dwelling need to be filled with worship before the owner fills them with His pres-ence and glory. We will never fill these temples with worship unless we prepare them His way. Our way doesn't reveal God's heart, but ours, which are wicked; our way doesn't show God's intentions, but ours, which are wicked. Our way doesn't show God's nature, but ours which are wicked. *"For my thoughts are not your thoughts, neither are your ways my ways, declares the Lord"* (Isa. 55:8).

When God told Moses to build the Tabernacle, He made clear that rules should be followed; not only during the construction of it, but also for the way to present sacrifices to Him and the way to approach His presence. Although this appears in the Old Testament, we can't neglect the pattern. Of course we live under a new covenant, made by the ultimate sacrifice of Jesus who shed His blood on the cross so we can be forgiven and redeemed from our sins, bringing us back to our original condition of God's image and likeness. But God is still holy, it is His nature, and He still is unable to dwell in an unholy temple. So we cannot expect His manifest presence when everything inside this temple is not in the accordance to His pattern. It is true that we can come to Jesus just as we are — dirty, broken, imperfect, full of sins — for He says, *"Come to me, all you who are weary and burdened, and I will give you rest."* (Matt. 11:28). But it is also true that once we come to Jesus, accepting His sacrifice and His Lordship, we are no longer people who just *bring* sacrifices for the priests to offer, we become priests of this new covenant, who *offer our own* sacrifices before God. *"You also, like living stones, are being built into a spiritual house to be a holy priesthood, offering spiritual sacrifices acceptable to God through Jesus Christ."* (1 Pet. 2:5). As priests, our obligation is to offer a pure sacrifice. *Therefore, I urge you, brothers, in view of God's mercy, to offer your bodies as living sacrifices, holy and pleasing to God; this is your spiritual act of worship.* (Rom. 12:1). More than that, we are at the same time His <u>temple.</u> *"For we are the temple of the living God."* (2 Cor. 6:16) and <u>priests</u> *"You are a chosen people, a royal priesthood a holy nation, a people belonging to God, that you may declare the praises of Him"* (1 Pet. 2:9). Everything needs to function together according to His heavenly pattern: a pure sacrifice, offered by a holy priest, in the place of God's dwelling.

Many may ask, "If I am the one who is offering the worship, why do I have to do it in God's way?"

The answer comes with another question. Does your way bring honor and glory to God? Of course only you and God can answer this question, and surely God knows the answer, but do you? Is your answer based on your feelings and thoughts? Or it is based on the assurance that your way is in accordance to the Word of God? When our way is not based on God's Word, we can worship however many times we want, we can continuously try but it will never bring glory to God. The only way to bring honor and glory to Him is by obeying and applying His Word.

In taking a closer look at today's spiritual application of the Tabernacle, we can clearly see that it remains an expression of the heavenly Tabernacle; a projection of us as a temple of God, places of His dwelling and places of worship. Therefore, our physical bodies with their ways of life and our worship must be connected to the ways of worship happening before the throne of our Lord. We must be an extension of His dwelling and an extension of the heavenly worship; both functions are completely interconnected, because without worship there is no manifested presence.

One of the first things revealed to us when we study the description of the Tabernacle is that before anything else, before any description of the utensils to be used in the sacrifices, before any description of the rituals of purification or sacrifices and offerings, before any details related to the construction itself, God told Moses to prepare the three most important pieces that would be indispensable inside the Tabernacle; the Ark of the Covenant, the table, and the lampstand. Without any one of these, the work of construction and the rituals of sacrifices and offerings would be in vain, for these three important pieces are the representation of the presence of God the Father, God the Son, and God the Holy Spirit. It is impossible to offer a true sacrifice of worship when one of them is missing. It is impossible to honor one and neglect another. It is impossible to say we worship God when we reject the work of the Holy Spirit. It is impossible to say we live a spiritual life when the Word (Jesus) is not part of our life. It is impossible to follow Jesus, when we have no desire to honor the Father. For Jesus said, *"I honor my father"* (John 8:49).

One simple and fundamental question comes to mind. Are we really on the right path when it comes to worshiping and honoring God? When I look back to my childhood in the church, I now understand the church, unintentionally, was off track in the way of worshiping God. Tradition kept me from discovering God's way of true worship, limiting my freedom of expression. Tradition denies the truth that says, *"If the Son sets you free, you will be free indeed."* (John 8:36). Tradition determines what, how and where you can or can't do or say something. This is legalism which can keep us from the relationship with Jesus through the Holy Spirit. It is so wonderful the way everything works together: God the Father planned true worship and God the Holy Spirit leads us to and through the Word (God the Son) to be true worshipers of the Triune God, because they are one. If we leave one of them out of this cycle, it means that we give up our position of worshiper of God to become worshipers of the evil one. Radical? Well . . . God is radical in His ways.

My traditional church in Brazil made no room for any kind of manifestation of the Holy Spirit, such as speaking in tongues or prophecy. Anything out of the routine of how the service was conducted would be forbidden, and if it came from a member of the church he or she would be subjected to reprehension. If it came from a visitor, he or she would be seen as a person who came to disturb the service. This didn't happen only in my church, but in all churches and groups that were part of the same denomination. In my late teen years I was involved in leadership of the state association for teenagers where we promoted an annual three-day statewide teen conference. On Saturday night we had a band from a church that was a little more progressive, the worship minister leading everybody in a different way to express our worship with dance, claps, and shouts of hallelujah. It was a great moment for us, but after the service, the leadership of the association was called by the leadership of the church, and we were told that type of worship was not allowed. We were so devastated. Although we felt we didn't do anything wrong, it was against their beliefs. "This is not the way we worship here. This is a traditional church. If people pass by on the street, they will think we are Pentecostal, and we don't want that."

Various denominations can have different points of view from different interpretations of the scriptures, but these cannot change the facts that we serve the same God, saved by the same Jesus, been bought by the same blood shed on the same cross 2,000 years ago. It also cannot change the fact that we are one body.

> *"There is one body and one Spirit. Just as you were called to one hope when you were called."* (Eph. 4:4).

> *"Just as a body, though one, has many parts, but all its many parts form one body, so it is in Christ."* (1 Cor. 12:12).

Even though denominations were created by man, I believe there is a purpose of God for us to have so many different denominations with differing points of view to appeal to and draw many different types and cultures of people. As long as these differences don't divide the body of Christ.

To illustrate: could feet say to our hands that what they are doing is wrong? Or if our eyes say to the nose that what it is doing is wrong? It is the same when we, belonging to one denomination, start to say that another denomination is wrong in their way of worship, or the ways they conduct their services or their interpretation of the Bible. 1 Corinthians 12:12 doesn't speak in the context of the local church, but it speaks to the Body of Christ, speaks to the Bride of Jesus. Jesus doesn't have multiple brides: Baptist bride, Presbyterian bride, Pentecostal bride . . . He has one bride: the Church. None of these denominations can define the perfect way of worship, for no man ever made a perfect way to worship or to serve our Lord. The perfect way is His way, and for me His way starts in our obedience to Him and His Word. There is no other way to please Him except with our obedience.

I love the passage of 1 Samuel 15:22. *"Does the Lord delight in burnt offerings and sacrifices as much as in obeying the Lord? To obey is better than sacrifice, and to heed is better than the fat of rams*. For me, this passage defines what worship is: obedience. There is no worship without obedience.

In the church of my youth, we didn't focus much on the power and gifts of the Holy Spirit. Their interpretation is that the gifts were only for the time of the apostles in order to expand the gospel; in the present age we have other ways to spread the gospel. This was also my thought at that time. But one thing I remember very clearly, we did focus on The Word. Everybody knew the word, which is a good thing, but without the Spirit, it is just knowledge. The same way, to focus on the power, the gifts and work of the Holy Spirit without knowledge and practice of the Word, is just temporary emotion. Both the Spirit and the Word need to be known and experienced together on the same level if we want to enter into the Holy of Holies, place of dwelling and worship of the Lord. That is why the Table of the Bread, representing the Word of God and the Fire of the Lampstand representing the Holy Spirit were in the same room inside the Tabernacle. They both have the same importance in our journey of worship.

Another point we should observe about ways of worship comes from worshiping in a multicultural community, specifically about how each culture expresses our worship to God and how each demonstrates joy in His presence. My current church has more than 35 nations represented, most of them from Africa. Coming from a part of Brazil where there is a big influence from the Africans gave me the chance to know a little about their culture, especially their dance. In Brazil they use the same dance as part of a cult called *"Umbanda"* or *"candomble,"* which is a kind of witchcraft that invokes demons to do all types of work for the people who call them. Whenever I saw this kind of dance, immediately I associated it to that cult. I could never visualize that type of dance in our traditional worship service because in my mind it was a way to call demons, and that was a sin. At that point in my life, I did not realize this was a common type of dance in their country, not only in that cult.

When we moved to the United States, we were introduced to people from all over the world. I remember when an African pastor friend of ours invited us to a service in his church—the first time my wife and I attended an African church. When we arrived, we heard the sound of worship. Their music, their language, their dance. It immediately took me back to my experience in Brazil, in a service in the Umbanda cult and the connection that I always made between the dance and the religion. But for the Africans it was a natural and a perfect way to express their joy in worship. If I started to judge them based on my old conception of that type of dance, and started to say that they were bringing evil and unauthorized elements to God's altar, I would be wrong.

I love to see people expressing, in an extravagant way, the joy of being in God's presence, the wonder of when saints run to the altar just to worship God with song, dance, lifted hands, shouts of joy, and hallelujahs. The fact is, it doesn't matter what I see, nor what I like to see, because what really matters is what God sees. When we see it from this perspective, we can say that it is also wonderful to see people expressing their worship in a quiet mode. God sees their hearts and their intentions; we see just the appearance, and the movements. Who is right? I vote for God.

In worship, we cannot use our opinions to show others how to worship, but we need to submit our conceptions to the Word, and then lead others through the true meaning of obedience in worship to become a true worshiper.

"The True Worshiper lays down his way, and worships God in God's way."

Chapter 8

THE POWER OF WORSHIP

"For the joy of the Lord is our strength."

(Neh. 8:10b)

T he power of worship. I've heard this expression my whole life from pastors, worship leaders, lay people, people who experienced this power in their lives, and from those who never experienced the power but repeated it by rote. Most of the time this expression is not fully understood, and because of this, power of worship remains unavailable for use. Hosea 4:6 alerts us, *"My people are destroyed from lack of knowledge . . ."* Therefore, it is imperative for us to acquire the knowledge of the Word of God to help us through the trials that life presents, which Jesus warned us about, *"I have told you these things, so that in me you may have peace. In this world you will have trouble. But take heart! I have overcome the world"*. (John 16:33)

I touched on this power generated by our worship in chapter two, when we saw it used as a weapon in spiritual warfare. King Jehoshaphat, in response to the Word of God, used worship to win the battle against the Moabites and the Ammonites.

Just like Jehoshaphat, we also need to be alert and discerning in our spirits to be open to the Word of God, for it is the Word that always will motivate us to worship. And only through the application of the Word of God will we be able to renew our minds, bringing the revelation of God into our hearts as scripture tells us in Romans 12:2. It is through the Word that we will grasp the knowledge to be able to understand the power of our worship. Without the Word we don't have faith, and without faith it is impossible to worship. When we fully understand that we were created to worship God before anything else, the pursuit of this power will be always in our hearts and minds.

Can this power change circumstances in our lives? Absolutely. Does it mean every time we go through bad moments and troubles in our lives, we can start to worship and everything, automatically, will be solved? Absolutely not. Therefore, where is this power of worship if I cannot reach it when I worship? What power is this if everything seems unchanged? This power is not only a weapon to eliminate trials in our lives, but one we can use as we go through troubles and trials. Through my worship, God may not take me out of the problem, but He surely takes me out of myself, bringing me into His dimension, where the problem cannot exist. Worship causes me to see everything in a spiritual perspective, through God's eyes. It is in the spiritual realm where we receive the strategies to deal with every problem that happens to us in the physical realm, but the most important power in our worship is in the transforming of ourselves, molding us, again, into God's image and likeness.

This type of worship is a lifestyle of walking in obedience to God.

In 2002 Daniella and I went to a Benny Hinn Conference. I had heard reports of how people were healed when he touched them; how people were filled by the Holy Spirit. I was amazed at his life.

Pastor Hinn's experiences motivated me to pursue the Holy Spirit and understand His work in my life. Even though I wanted the flowing of the Holy Spirit in my life, I still was skeptical about it being available to post-apostle Christianity. During the conference a glorious atmosphere of praise and worship preceded Benny Hinn's entrance on the stage—but nobody acknowledged it! There was no announcement, he just came and entered into the worship atmosphere filling the place. In the midst of worship people started to receive healings: the deaf heard, the lame walked. Pastor Hinn didn't touch anyone, but the presence of God, who was, is, and always will dwell in the midst of the praises of His people, started to put everything that was out of order in people's bodies back to normal. But I still had doubts about what was happening, because in my mind I thought, "those people in wheelchairs never needed them; those people who indicated they were deaf were not. Everything was arranged." But God had a purpose when He sent me there—to show me that He is still the same. The same God who talks, heals and who does miracles. I realized that when a little boy, about four years old, was healed. He was taken to the stage, Benny Hinn touched him and the little boy fell to the ground. A four-year old child would never lie about that. In that moment God changed my perception about the Holy Spirit. Another thing I realized; worship doesn't heal; worship doesn't perform miracles. Worship draws the presence of God, and that is when miracles happen. It's not a pastor's performance or preaching, not singing or playing an instrument, but its God's presence that puts our lives in true perspective, on the true path to achieve the purpose He has for us. Worship is a journey of acknowledgment of God, a journey of intimacy with God. The more I worship Him, the more His presence will be tangible in my life. The more His presence is tangible in my life, the more I will be like Him. That is the power I want in my life. The way we can appropriate it is worshiping God in Spirit and Truth. *"Yet a time is coming and has now come when the true worshipers will worship the Father in spirit and truth, for this is the kind of worshipers the Father is looking for."* (John 4:23)

Our worship is very powerful to change circumstances, to break the chains that bind us and prevent us from flowing in the Spirit, to bring order to the chaos of our lives. Perhaps the greatest power we can find in our worship is the transformation that takes place in the life of the worshiper. We see this in the life of the patriarch, Abraham.

While still Abram, he feared death by the Egyptians.

"When the Egyptians see you, they will say, this is his wife. Then they will kill me but will let you live." (Gen. 12:12).

But now, as Abraham, he had the conviction that God could raise Isaac, his son of the promise, from the dead.

> *"Abraham reasoned that God could raise the dead, and figuratively speaking, he did receive Isaac back from death."* (Heb. 11:19).

What changed Abraham from accepting the riches from pharaoh to the conviction that Abraham's riches would come from the Lord when he refused to receive anything from the king of Sodom?

> *"(Pharaoh) treated Abram well for her sake, and Abram acquired sheep and cattle, male and female donkeys, menservants and maidservants, and camels."* (Gen. 12:16).

> *"But Abram said to the king of Sodom, I have raised my hand to the Lord God Most High, Creator of heaven and earth, and have taken an oath that I will accept nothing belonging to*

you, not even a thread or the thong of a sandal,

so that you will never be able to say, I made

Abram rich." (Gen. 14:22–23).

When we study the life of Abraham, we see a constant, growing relationship between him and God; a constant growing lifestyle of worship, building altars, and letting God transform him to the point where Abraham chose believing God and His promise. Even though Abraham made mistakes along the way, had moments of doubts, moments when he preferred to listen to other voices than God's, moments of agony and questions, in the end he believed God to make good on His promise about an heir through Sarah.

"But Abram said, O Sovereign Lord, what can

you give me since I remain childless and the

one who will inherit my estate is Eliezer of

Damascus? You have given me no children; so

a servant in my household will be my heir."

(Gen. 15:2–3).

"So (Sarai) said to Abram, The Lord has kept

me from having children. Go, sleep with my

maidservant; perhaps I can build a family

through her." (Gen. 16:2).

"Then God said, "Take your only son Isaac,
whom you love, and go to the region of Moriah.
Sacrifice him there as a burnt offering on one
of the mountains I will tell you about."

(Gen. 22:2).

Abraham stayed in the journey. While many may believe he pursued the promise, he pursued the one whose voice he heard. Can you imagine living in a place full of gods, where none could talk, and suddenly you hear a voice telling you, *"leave your country . . . I will bless you . . . I will make you a great nation . . . go to a place I will show you."* (Gen. 12:1–2). At that time Abram knew nothing about God, but the voice he heard must have caused a desire to know the One who talked to him, called him, guided him, protected him, and blessed him.

If that is so, then what caused Abram to fear and tell lies? It is what happens to us all. We are humans. One day we heard the voice of the Holy Spirit and we decided to follow Jesus. And even after this we, too, still make mistakes, we still lie, we still fear, we still try to do things our way, and we still listen to other voices. But as long as we continue pursuing Him and our relationship with Him, the bumps along life's way will become less and less until we find ourselves looking just like Him at the end of our journey.

Even myself, taught by my parents to follow God and to do His will, grew up in church, living in an atmosphere where everyone around me talked about God and how we need to submit ourselves to Him, there was a day when the God of my parents called me to establish my own commitment and relationship with Him. When I said yes to Him, He became *my* God. Only then did I start to hear Him for myself, follow Him as my God, worship Him and experience the power of worship in my life.

Our own individual decisions, journeys and experiences are exactly what makes each of our worship experiences so unique. My parents' worship never gave me intimacy with God. Their worship wouldn't have had any effect in my life if I hadn't decided to worship Him too. My parents' worship made them look like Him. My worship makes *me* look like Him. Consider the words from king David to his son Solomon:

> "And you, my son Solomon, acknowledge the God of your father, and serve Him with whole-hearted devotion and with a willing mind, for the Lord searches every heart, and understands every motive behind the thoughts. If you seek Him, he will be found by you; but if you forsake Him, He will reject you forever."
> (1 Chron. 28:9).

It is true we can't ignore the fact that our decisions, either to submit ourselves to God or not, giving Him the worship

He deserves or not, affect our generations to come. There will always be a need for our descendants to establish their own covenant of worship with God, to pursue their own intimacy and experiences with Him.

> *"As for you (Solomon), if you walk before me in integrity of heart and uprightness, as David your father did, and do all commands and observe my decrees and laws, I will establish your royal throne over Israel forever, as I promised David your father when I said: You shall never fail to have a man on the throne of Israel."*   (2 Kings 9:4–5).

> *"The Lord became angry with Solomon because his heart had turned away from the Lord, the God of Israel, who had appeared to him twice . . . So the Lord said to Solomon, 'since this is your attitude and you have not kept my covenant and my decrees, which I commanded you, I will most certainly tear the kingdom away from you and give it to one of your subordinates. Nevertheless, for the sake of David your father, I will not do it during your lifetime. I will tear it out of the hand of your son.'"*   (1 Kings 11:9–12).

David's worship made him a man after God's heart, a man who united and established the kingdom of Israel; the lack of worship and disobedience from Solomon and his son, Rehoboam, tore the kingdom apart.

At the close of this chapter, what we need to comprehend is that the power of worship is still available to us; after all, worship is the weapon God gives us to fight the enemy. But no weapon has power if it is never used. And the choice to use it is each of ours, individually.

"A True Worshiper is transformed everyday by the power of his worship, into the fullness image of God."

Chapter 9

CALLED TO WORSHIP

*"You will be for me a kingdom of priests and a
holy nation."* (Ex. 19:6)

*"But you are a chosen people, a royal priest-
hood, a holy nation, a people belonging to
God, that you may declare the praises of Him
who called you out of darkness into his wonderful light."* (1 Pet. 2:9)

W hat a great privilege for us to have been called to
come before the throne of the Most High, ministering in worship. All believers are part of this calling. It
doesn't matter what the ministry: children, marriage, missions, pastor, teacher, worship or any other leader in your
church. These are functions that are necessary in the Church
*"to prepare God's people for works of service, so that the
body of Christ may be built up until we all reach unity in*

faith and in the knowledge of the Son of God and become mature, attaining to the whole measure of the fullness of Christ." (Eph. 4:12–13).

When we talk about worship in Spirit and Truth, it is not about a function in the church, but about the expression of our love to God. This type of worship is not a ministry, but a calling. When we name it a ministry, we start to exclude some people, especially because of the tendency to associate worship with music. According to that reasoning, if someone is not included in the worship team, he or she has no active roll in the worship. But when we understand it as a calling, we ascribe to it the totally different meaning of inclusiveness to it. In thinking this way, we worship while we work in the children ministry; we worship while we work in the marriage ministry; we worship while we work with missions; we worship while we fulfill our pastoral calling; we worship while we teach; we worship while we sing, play an instrument, or dance. We worship simply because we are called to do so— created to do so. Music does have an important role to play in the Church; it is part of the amazing expression of our worship, powerful and beautiful.

Whether you are a worship leader or not, we all share the same call: to offer a sacrifice of worship before God.

When God chose and set apart the people of Israel, they were to be a kingdom of priests and a holy nation through whom all the other nations of the earth would be blessed, keeping the promise He made to Abraham, *"You will be for me a kingdom of priests and a holy nation . . ."* (Ex. 19:6). A kingdom of priests where everyone, with no exceptions, would come before God, stand in His presence with no guilt or sin, to fellowship with Him and worship Him. That through the example of Israel's worship, all the other nations would be able to do the same. This is the blessing for all the nations: reconciliation with God.

God's plan wasn't only for the Old Testament, or just for the people of Israel. In the New Testament, He also calls us to be part of it. And like it was in the past with Israel, God requires from us the same obedience; it is more than just having Jesus as our savior. We need to surrender to Him as Lord, ready and willing to do anything and everything He tells us to do. Obedience is the key to fulfill this purpose of God for our lives. Just as it happened to Israel in the past, when only the tribe of Levi was committed enough to do whatever God ordered, then they were set apart to be the tribe of priests, it still happens today. Obedience is the key to be part of God's purpose.

> *"Then he said to them, this is what the Lord, God of Israel says: Each man strap a sword to his side. Go back and forth through the camp from one end to the other, each killing his brother and friend and neighbor. The Levites did as Moses commanded, and that day about three thousand of the people died.*

Then Moses said, you have been set apart to
the Lord today, for you were against your own
sons and brothers, and He has blessed you
this day."   (Ex. 32:27–29).

Many Christians prefer to believe that after the Cross there is no need to repent and purify themselves nor to offer sacrifices before our Lord. Romans 12:1 tells us to *"offer our bodies as a living sacrifice, holy before God."*

"But you are a chosen people, a royal priest-
hood, a holy nation, a people belonging to
God, that you may declare the praises of Him
who called you out of darkness into his won-
derful light."   (1 Pet. 2:9)

"All this is from God, who reconciled us to
Himself through Christ and gave us the min-
istry of reconciliation: that God was rec-
onciling the world to Himself in Christ, not
counting men's sins against them. And He
has committed to us the message of reconcil-
iation."   (2 Cor. 5:18–19)

"Now, if you obey me fully and keep my cov-
enant, then out of all nations you will be my
treasured possession. Although the whole

earth is mine, you will be for me a kingdom
of priests and a holy nation." (Ex. 19:5–6).

God's plan is to reconcile the whole world to Him, and we are part of this plan. As priests of the new covenant, our lives need to be instruments of this reconciliation between God and mankind. Without full obedience this will never happen.

LEADING WORSHIP

God gave me amazing revelations for my role as a worship leader, which changed my perspective about my relationship with God as a worshiper who wants to worship Him in Spirit and Truth.

WHAT ARE YOU LISTENING TO?

One day I was at a twenty-four hour worship event in Connecticut, and I heard this statement from the pastor who was hosting the event, that made me consider what type of music we, as God's people, are listening to. *"Music has the power to take you to the place where it was created."* Where have you been taken? Where do you find inspiration to write a new song or do a new guitar solo? There are only two places where music is created. In God, the creator of everything, and in Lucifer (the devil), who was created with music inside of him. *"You were in Eden, the garden of God; every precious*

stone was your covering . . . The workmanship of your tim-
brels (or tambourines), and pipes was prepared for you on
the day you were created." (Ezek. 28:13 NKJV).

Music was created inside of Lucifer. The sound of every
kind of instrument, every rhythm that we know—and those
we don't know yet—everything related to music was created
inside of him. I believe beautiful melodies were formed with
his walk, with the waving of his arms, with the moving of
his head. I believe the songs of worship that came out of him
made him the most beautiful angelical being in the kingdom
of heaven. But the same music that made him this unique,
most beautiful angel, was also the reason he thought he could
be like God and so rebelled against Him.

That is why I am concerned about what kind of music
God's people are listening to. Your objection may be, "Come
on! There are songs that are not Christian, but they are not
demonic either." My understanding is this: Music was created
to praise God, and Lucifer used the music inside of him to do
so. When he thought in his heart he should be praised because
of the beauty reflected by his music, he became prideful,
thinking that he should be praised. If God is not praised nor
honored through your song, who is? The devil? You? What
are you looking for through your music? To worship God
or to get attention, recognition, fame? When musicians seek
fame and recognition through music, they fall into the same
sin into which Lucifer fell.

We need to be careful of what music we allow into our spirits, where we go to prepare ourselves to lead the worship at church. As we sing we are declaring the words of the song, not only in the physical realm, but especially in the spiritual realm. As we listen to a song, our spirits and souls are being ministered to by the words. There is a big difference between declaring the words of a song and declaring the Word of God that is transmitted by the words of a song. There is a big difference between letting our hearts be ministered to by the words of a song, and letting our hearts be ministered to by the Word of God that is transmitted by the words of a song. A song that contains only words and not the Word of God will never be able to please God, because it wasn't created in Him. The thought that there's nothing wrong in listening to music created outside God has infiltrated into the minds of many Christians, compromising their faith, their convictions, and their ability to offer to the Lord holy, true, and spiritual worship. I am unable to spend my days listening to songs that were not created in the Lord, filling up my heart, mind, and soul, and expect to come to church on Sunday and present my worship to God. How can I express to God what is in my heart and my mind after filling them with music that doesn't exalt nor praise Him, but praises the devil or people? Worship is the expression of what is in the heart. Worshiping in Spirit and Truth is the expression of a heart who lives in the Spirit and in Truth.

This is a testimony of a friend of mine: early in my Christian life, God asked me to put down all secular music because even lovely music combined with ungodly words, would get stuck in my head (now referred to as an "earworm") and I would sing those songs or it would play "in the background," and I would concentrate on that, taking my thoughts to a place I should not dwell on.

At the time of the restoration of our marriage, Daniella and I made a covenant together, and with God, that in our home no music would be played except Christian music. Sometimes we leave songs of worship playing for one whole week or more. When we move to a new house, we leave songs of worship playing for at least for a month. We constantly fill our home with songs that honor, exalt, and worship our God, so not only us, but our daughters, and everyone who comes to our house will always be ministered to by the music playing. We have friends who say that the atmosphere in our house is so peaceful, so Godly. I truly believe that when we, as a family, decided to honor God in our home, He transformed not only us, but also the place we live.

DON'T RELY ON YOUR ABILITY

"Not that we are competent in ourselves to claim anything for ourselves, but our competence comes from God. He has made us competent as ministers of a new covenant, not of

the letter but of the Spirit; for the letter kills,
but the Spirit gives life."   (2 Cor. 3:5–6).

You or I might be an extraordinary singer or guitar player; you or I might have a talent to lead God's people in worship better than anyone else. It feels good to see the church responding in worship when we are leading. It feels good when people come to us and tell us that we did it well and the worship was powerful. How do our spirits respond to these types of comments? How do we feel when this happens? How do we feel when this doesn't happen?

During my time leading worship in church, I've worked with all levels and qualities of singers and musicians: amateurs, professionals, some who sang out of tune, some extraordinary, some not so extraordinary. We should always strive for excellence in everything we do, to push hard to offer our best to our Lord. I don't concern myself with that. Is worship just about our technique, our ability to play and sing? Does really matter in our worship?

A few years ago, when ministering with a worship team, they complained that no matter how much they practiced, no matter how good they played, the church didn't respond eagerly to the worship they were leading. I listened to every complaint and asked two simple questions, Do you worship at home? Do you spend time alone with God? To my surprise the answer was the same from all of them. "No, I don't have time!" How can we expect to lead the church in something we don't experience?

How can we expect something from others if we don't discipline ourselves to do what God expects from us? I have this assurance in my heart—that I don't need to please anyone but God with the expression of my worship. And I know that my talent, my ability to play instruments, my singing, my time spent in practicing will never make me a true worshiper, but my heart will. None of these things will be the key to move the congregation in worship. This is an exclusive job of the Holy Spirit. We just need to seek Him, and let Him act.

A worship team doesn't have to worry whether or not the church is joining them in worship. When the team does that, they are taking the responsibility to make the people worship; they are saying that the worship is about them. When a worship team relies only on their talents, it says that the worship is about them. The danger is that they may fall into the same sin as Lucifer. Through our lives and through our calling we lead the people in worship, but the one who moves and leads their hearts to worship is the Holy Spirit, and the decision to worship and let the Holy Spirit flow in their lives is theirs. Our responsibility is just to fulfill our calling, which is to worship the Lord.

HOW IS YOUR LIFE?

As we stand before God in worship and before the congregation leading the people in worship, one thing should always come to mind. Is my life right before God? Is my life a Godly example? In the Old Testament, the life of the high priest and the sacrifices he made could be a blessing or a curse to the people. If God accepted the sacrifice, it meant the people had one more year of forgiveness and blessings. If God didn't accept the sacrifice, the people wouldn't have God's forgiveness nor His blessings. The same is true of our lives as worship leaders. God gave me the understanding that improper worship could/would lead to a curse.

In the first chapter, I mentioned that Lucifer and Adam had important positions, leading worship and praises to God, and then they decided to rebel against God. Have prideful thoughts ever come to your mind when you were leading the worship? Let's look at an example from my own life.

When I was studying the temptation of Jesus by the devil in the wilderness, God revealed something new to me. The devil constantly tempts us to rebel against God, but when we are in a position of leading the people to God, the devil always pushes harder. He knows if the leader falls, many others will fall with him. This is what Lucifer did in heaven, and a third part of the angels fell with him. Adam also rebelled and all succeeding generations were born with a sin nature and the earth itself was cursed because of him. *"Cursed is the ground because of you."* (Gen. 3:17). The devil tried to make Jesus fall so there would never be a perfect sacrifice to substitute for sin; everyone would be lost forever. The devil still uses the same temptations he did with Adam and Jesus. One fell, the other overcame the temptation. If we fall, many in the congregation may fall with us.

Jesus started His ministry being led by the Holy Spirit to be tempted by the devil. What a strange way to start your calling. There is a tendency to think that if the Holy Spirit leads, there will be no temptation. The Bible says, *"Live by the Spirit, and you will not gratify the desires of the sinful nature."* (Gal. 5:16). This doesn't say we will have no temptations, but that we will overcome them. When we allow ourselves to be led into temptation, the result will not be a positive one.

Have you ever had a check in your spirit where the voice of the God whispers to you, "Don't go there." And you ignore the voice and argue that you are strong and won't fall! Later you ask yourself, "Why did I go there, why did I do that?" Thinking that we won't fall because we are worship leaders is foolishness; thinking we can handle the temptation just because of our position is foolishness. I can guarantee that many of these temptations come in our minds when we are in front of the congregation leading the worship.

I can relate the temptation of Jesus to the battles we have as worship leaders.

Jesus knew his ministry was not about Him, but about doing the Father's will. So it is with the worship ministry. We don't need to be seen to fulfill this calling of leading worship; we don't need to prove it to anybody, especially to the devil. When we know who we are in Jesus, we understand that everything is about Him and doing His will.

"If you are the Son of God, tell these stones to
become bread." (Matt. 4:3b)

When the devil told Jesus to transform stones into bread, he was tempting Jesus to use His power for His own benefit. The devil also tempts us in this way. We need to realize God didn't call us to bless ourselves through our calling, but He called us with one purpose in mind; to be an instrument of reconciliation. *"All this is from God, who reconciled us to Himself through Christ and gave us the ministry of reconciliation."* (2 Cor. 2:18). Our call may be to worship and lead worship, but our ministry is definitely to reconcile the world with God.

"Then the devil took Him to the holy city and
had Him stand on the highest point of the
temple. If you are the Son of God, he said,
throw yourself down, for it is written: He will
command his angels concerning you, and they
will lift you up in their hands, so that you will
not strike your foot against a stone."
(Matt. 4:5–6).

The devil tried to place in Jesus' heart the same thing that made the devil fall—pride. I've seen this happen to many members of worship teams. The power to do something amazing, something that nobody else could do, and knowing that you would get all the attention, and praise for that, is very tempting. If we are not aware, we can become a serious candidate for a fall because of this temptation. Many musicians and worship leaders don't consider themselves as instruments, but as artists. Artists seek recognition while instruments just want to be used. We are instruments set apart to be used by God to bring honor and praises to Him, not to ourselves.

There is always a fine line that can take us to pride if we don't stay vigilant. The first step in resisting temptation is recognizing that the congregation is not an audience. Words from our mouths can appear very humble, transferring all the praises we receive to God, while our heart, quietly, receives the honor, telling us we deserve it. I know this is true, because it happened to me. When I became aware of how and why those temptations came, I was able to overcome the temptation of pride just like Jesus did—with the Word.

> *"Humble yourselves before the Lord, and He will lift you up."* (James 4:10).

> *"For whoever exalts himself will be humbled, and whoever humbles himself will be exalted."* (Matt. 23:1.2)

> *"You are worthy, our Lord and God, to receive glory and honor . . ."* (Rev. 4:11).

"For they loved praise from men more than praise from God." (John 12:43).

"For yours is the kingdom and the power and the glory forever amen." (Matt. 6:13 NKJV).

"Therefore, as it is written: Let him who boasts boast in the Lord." (1 Cor. 1:31).

"May I never boast except in the cross of our Lord Jesus Christ, through which the world has been crucified to me, and I to the world. (Gal. 6:14).

"In God we make our boast all day long, and we will praise your name forever." (Ps. 44:8).

Worship leaders, like everyone else, need to always ask God to check the motives of our hearts. *"Search me, oh God, and know my heart; test me and know my anxious thoughts."* (Ps. 139:23). Where are our hearts? If our hearts are drawn to performing in front of a congregation, and not in worshiping God, we have already fallen into the temptation of pride, and fail God in our call as worshipers, to the church as ministers of the altar, and to ourselves as instruments of reconciliation between man and God.

"For where your treasure is, there your heart will be also." (Matt. 6:21).

"Above all, guard your heart, for it is the well-spring of life." (Prov. 4:23).

"The heart is deceitful above all things and beyond cure." (Jer. 17:9).

I continually ask God to guard my heart from the trap of accolades. Even when there is applause, I pray that my heart will not receive it; when there is praise, I pray that my heart will continue to be humble. And if even a fleeting thought of receiving honor from men for feeling special for doing what God called me to do comes to my mind, I pray that I will always be able to nail it to the cross, bringing this thought captive to making it obedient to Christ. *"Again, the devil took Him to a very high mountain and showed Him all the kingdoms of the world and their splendor. All this I will give you, he said, if you will bow down and worship me."* (Matt. 4:8–9).

The battle we are in is about worship; everything the devil invests against us is to bring us over to his side and to stop our worship to God. The devil will try to make us use our talents to glorify him. Understand that our God never changes, nor does His nature. *"I the Lord do not change."* (Mal. 3:6). When we talk about God's nature and character, it is so easy for us to focus on his love, mercy, goodness, holiness, righteousness, and all the good things that we know are related to Him. It is inconceivable for us to think that jealousy is an attribute of God. We see jealousy as a negative attribute, a characteristic of an insecure and selfish person, and these characteristics could have nothing to do with God. We want to assume that everything about Him is positive. The reality is that God is a jealous God, and every time this statement appears in the Bible it has to do with worship. God is jealous for us, and it's not okay with Him for us to take the talents He gave us to worship Him and use them to exalt the enemy in worship.

"You shall not bow down to (idols) or worship them; for I, the Lord your God, am a jealous God." (Ex. 20:5).

"Do not worship any other god, for the Lord, whose name is jealous, is a jealous God." (Ex. 34:14).

"Be careful not to forget the covenant of the Lord your God that He made with you; do not make for yourselves an idol in the form of anything the Lord your God has forbidden. For the Lord your God is a consuming fire, a jealous God." (Deut. 4:23–24).

*"You cannot drink the cup of the Lord and the
cup of demons too; you cannot have a part in
both the Lord's table and the table of demons.
Are we trying to arouse the Lord's jealousy?
Are we stronger the He?"* (1 Cor. 10:21–22).

*"I am the Lord; that is my name. I will not give
my glory to another, or my praise to idols."*
(Isa. 42:8).

The Bible says in Luke 16:13, *"No servant can serve two masters. Either he will hate the one and love the other, or he will be devoted to the one and despise the other. You cannot serve both God and money."* The moment we decide to use our musical talents outside of God's kingdom with the intention to acquire fame and wealth, we are falling into the temptation of despising God and loving money. We know so many artists that started in faith, singing to the Lord in churches, worshiping Him with their beautiful voices and wonderful talents, but somewhere they were tempted and trapped by the opportunity of a career of fame and its riches. They won the world, but they lost the presence of God. They filled theaters and stadiums, but they lost the audience that matters—the audience of The One.

We are not entertainers. We are worship leaders who are here to lead people to the One who deserves all the glory and worship—Yahweh, The Great I AM. It is part of our fallen sin nature to seek recognition, but it is part of our new-born nature to humble ourselves and declare, like John the Baptist, *"He must become greater; I must become less."* (John 3:30). We can choose what to do. Either allow our sin nature to rule us, or embrace our new born nature. *"Everything is permissible for me, but not everything is beneficial. Everything is permissible for me but I will not be mastered by anything."* (1 Cor. 6:12).

There is a battle—the battle of and for worship—where worship is not only the reason, but the weapon. Running from this battle is not an option. We all are in the battle, whether we want to be or not. Using the weapon of worship God gave us is the only way for to finish victoriously. Your pastor cannot wield it for you, your spouse cannot, nobody else can use it for you. It is your choice.

"A true worshiper recognizes he is called to bring honor, glory, fame and worship to the only one who deserves it: Yahweh."

ABOUT THE AUTHOR

B orn in Brazil, Uziel Goncalves began to play the guitar at church when he was nine years old, and since then he's been always involved in Worship Ministry. He moved to the United States in 2000 with his wife Daniella, where after they overcame troubles in their marriage, they began to teach about Worship 24/7 as the only way of life. They've been married for twenty-two years, and both were ordained as Pastors in 2008. They serve at CCF Ministries in Lowell-MA, where they live with their two daughters Rachel and Deborah.

Contact:

Uziel G. Goncalves

ugaldino@hotmail.com

www.choosetoworship.com

CPSIA information can be obtained at www.ICGtesting.com
Printed in the USA
BVOW06s0337140916

462044BV00004B/9/P